Umbria

Other books by James Bentley

Albert Schweitzer
Alsace
Between Marx and Christ
The Blue Guide to Germany and Berlin
A Calendar of Saints
A Children's Bible
A Guide to the Dordogne
A Guide to Tuscany
Languedoc
Life and Food in the Dordogne
The Loire
Martin Niemöller
Normandy
Oberammergau and the Passion Play
The Rhine
Ritualism and Politics in Victorian Britain
Secrets of Mount Sinai
Weekend Cities

UMBRIA

James Bentley

AURUM PRESS

This book is dedicated to
Emma Louise Davson

First published 1989 by Aurum Press Limited,
33 Museum Street, London WC1A 1LD
Copyright © 1989 by James Bentley

Map by Richard Natkiel Associates
Illustration by Joy FitzSimmons

The author and publishers are grateful to the following
for permission to reproduce illustrations: Susan Griggs
Agency Ltd, nos 5 (Roslav Szaybo), 9 (John G. Ross);
John Sims, nos 3, 4, 6, 7, 8, 10; Zefa Picture Library
(U K) Ltd, nos 1 (K. Benser), 2 (Panda Photo).

The extract from 'Mr Eliot's Sunday Morning Service'
is reproduced by kind permission of Faber and Faber Ltd,
from *Collected Poems 1909–1962* by T. S. Eliot.

ISBN 1 85410 025 4

British Library Cataloguing in Publication Data

Bentley, James, *1937–*
Umbria
1. Umbria. Italy – Visitors' guides
I. Title
914.5'6504928

Typeset by Wyvern Typesetting Ltd, Bristol
Printed in Great Britain by The Bath Press, Avon

Contents

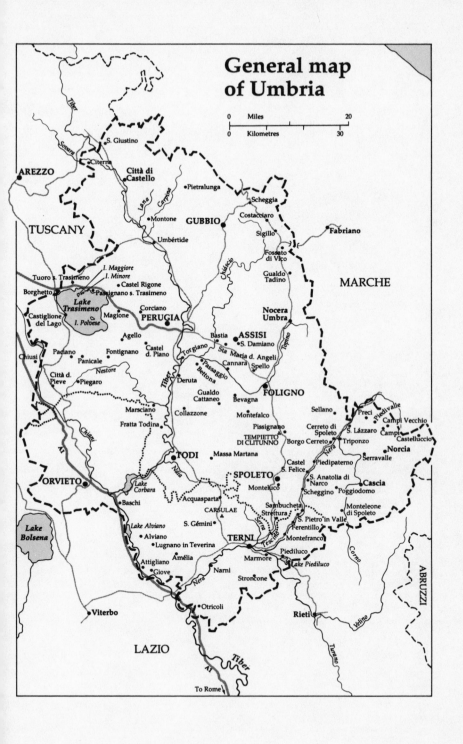

General map
of Umbria

Miles 0 — 20
Kilometres 0 — 30

Tiber

Scoora

S. Giustino
Citerna

AREZZO

Città di
Castello

Pietralunga

Scheggia

Lana

Carpina

Montone

GUBBIO

Costacciaro

Sigillo

Fabriano

TUSCANY

Umbértide

Fossato
di Vico

Gualdo
Tadino

MARCHE

Chiascio

I. Maggiore
I. Minore
Tuoro s. Trasimeno
Castel Rigone
Borghetto
Passignano s. Trasimeno
Lake
Trasimeno
Corciano
Castiglione
del Lago
I. Polvese
Magione
PERUGIA

Nocera
Umbra

Topino

Agello
Bastia
ASSISI
S. Damiano

Paciano
Fontignano
Castel
d. Piano
Torgiano
Sta Maria d. Angeli
Spello

Chiusi
Panicale
Nestore
Passaggio
Cannara

Città d.
Pieve
Piegaro
Bettona
Deruta

Marsciano
Gualdo
Cattaneo
Bevagna
FOLIGNO

Chiani
Fratta Todina
Collazzone
Montefalco
Sellano
Preci
Piedivalle

Al
Pissignano
Cerreto di
Spoleto
S. Lázzaro
Campi Vecchio
Campi
Castelluccio

Naia
Marsciano
TEMPIETTO
DI CLITUNNO
Borgo Cerreto
Triponzo
Serravalle
NORCIA

ORVIETO
TODI
Massa Martana
Nera

Baschi
Lake
Corbara
SPOLETO
Castel
S. Felice
Piedipaterno

Acquasparta
Monteluco
S. Anatolia di
Narco
Cascia

Lake Alviano
CARSULAE
Scheggino
Poggiodomo

Alviano
S. Gémini
Sambucheta
Strettura
Monteleone
di Spoleto

Lugnano in Teverina
Amélia
S. Pietro in Valle
Ferentillo

Attigliano
Montefranco
Corno

Giove
Nera
Narni
Marmore
Piediluco
Lake Piediluco

TERNI

Stroncone
Rieti
Velino

Piediluco

Otricoli

Lake
Bolsena

ABRUZZI

Viterbo
Rieti

Turano

LAZIO

Nera

Al
Tiber

To Rome

Preface

In 1866 Robert Browning confessed to a friend, 'My liking for Italy was always a selfish one – I felt alone with my soul there.' Browning added something I myself would never want to say: 'I shall not go to Florence again', and then said plaintively, 'I should like to have earned a few years of that sort of solitude somewhere else.'

Umbria is a region where, if you wish, you can certainly feel alone with your soul. Outside its matchless, majestic hill cities, with their bustling restaurants and piazze and their elegant citizens clattering down the cobblestones of the ancient streets, ranges of awesome mountains interplay with secluded river valleys, gentle pastures and quiet towns. Sometimes you drive past little stream-washed fortresses, now restored as homes. Other ruined castles peer forlornly from the tops of hills, down which walled villages tumble. A flag waving from another fortress tells you that someone still lives there.

The countryside is speckled with hidden towns and ancient villages whose farmers harvest grapes and olives from the slopes around their homes. Umbria is also indelibly permeated with the holy savour of St Francis of Assisi – Francis blessing the animals, telling the swallows to shut up while he preaches, converting a wolf to Christianity. Again and again inside the humblest Romanesque church a ravishing fresco by an Umbrian master will take you by surprise.

After a prologue conveying the flavour of the Umbrians themselves, as well as the succulence of their tables, the next five chapters of my book each begin with one of the five great Umbrian cities: Assisi, Perugia, Orvieto, Spoleto and Gubbio. I describe a tour of each city, designed to reveal the varied impact of Umbria's long history and its rich culture, as well as the modern delights of these places. Then each chapter leaves these cities for one or more entrancing tours of the oases of peace, and for the smiling towns and hamlets in the surrounding countryside.

Finally I attempt to sum up the essence of Umbria, no doubt an impossibility in a few thousand words. My book of course aims to prompt readers to see for themselves or, if they already relish Umbria, to go there again. It will be more useful if you use its index, wherever you are, for some spots in Umbria are so rich in folklore, art, food and history that I found it impossible to cram everything I wanted to say about them into one reference.

There are friends I must thank – first of all Jennifer Paton, PR Director of the Magic of Italy, 47 Shepherd's Bush Green, London W12 8PS, who, as previously, has been of enormous help to me. Jane Andersen, the Magic of Italy's representative in Umbria, and her husband Tommy went out of their way to show me much I would otherwise have missed and I here record my debt to both of them. Without their help I should not have discovered, or eaten at, the Hotel San Valentino, Todi.

The Magic of Italy also arranged my stay at the Hotel Gattapone, Spoleto, at the Hotel Bosone Palace, Gubbio, at Le Tre Vaselle, Torgiano, and in the countryside outside Assisi at the Hotel Silve di Armenzano.

I am also in various ways greatly indebted to Dottore Giuseppe Agozzino, Director of the Azienda di Promozione Turistica, Perugia; to Signora Simone Fanelli of Promotour Umbria, Perugia; to Signor Guiglio Hanke of the Hotel

Preface

Gattapone, Spoleto; to the Azienda Autonoma di Soggiorno e Turismo, Gubbio; to Signor Giancarlo Ronci, Director of the Azienda di Promozione Turistica, Assisi; and to Mandy Greenfield of Aurum Press (herself a lover of Umbria).

Here too I must express my gratitude to Signorina Paola Greco of the Italian National Tourist Board in London. Finally, I have greatly depended on my wife's patience and help in exploring this entrancing region of Italy.

James Bentley
FEBRUARY 1989

A *farm outside Assisi*

I could not make out whether Mario's thumb was coloured a deep black from the rich Umbrian soil or a blood-red from the grapes whose last dregs he was squeezing into a press. A week earlier Jane and Tommy Andersen had called on me to say that their friends the Bocciani family, of which Mario is the patriarch, were to press the last of that year's grapes and celebrate the wine festival with a family feast to which the Andersens had been invited. They had also enticed the Boccianis to invite me as well.

We arrived early, driving from my hotel to the farm on a hill outside Assisi. Countless barrels and funnel-shaped casks littered the farmyard, many turned on their sides. Two chained dogs yapped excitedly at us. Their puppies, roaming loose in the farmyard, leapt all over me as I got out of the car, though fortunately the sun was hot and their paws unmuddied. A huge Alsatian, dozing in the shade of the main farmhouse, refused even to move. Two wizened old grannies peered down at us all from a balcony, saying not a word in spite of my instant, if slightly hesitant, '*buon giorno*'. Under the flight of steps leading to their balcony stood a rickety work-bench with a modern vice. Washing hung on poles. Seemingly abandoned equipment rusted all around us. Chickens and pigeons spread their droppings in the yard.

1

Three fat pigs lay in a sty next to hemmed-in guinea fowl. I peered into the cool cow-shed and made out three puppies, two kittens and their mother.

In spite of the heat, a mist had not yet dispersed in the deeply cleft valley overlooked by the farm, and all that yet emerged from the cloud were the blue distant mountains. Signor Mario, who had never met me before, grinned delightedly, paused momentarily from his work at the wine-press and extended his black-red hand. Instantly I felt at ease.

The men wore wellington boots or sandals, the sandal-clad one without socks. Mario's task was to break up the remains of grapes already pressed, spreading them in the wine-press for a second time to extract the last drop of juice. What a drop! His red-haired, moustachioed son, Guiseppe, was briefly introduced to me, told me to call him Pepe and filled me a glass of the juice as it poured out of the press, crying one single word, '*dolce*'. Dulcet it was.

Mario's and Pepe's wives were working harder than their menfolk, carrying plastic buckets of red wine juice from the press and pouring it into barrels which lay on their side in a shady barn. In the disputes about the best way to extract the last drop of juice – disputes which abruptly filled the air with horrendous noise and almost immediately quietened down – the women were quite equal to the men. Bottles and buckets of grape juice were swiftly and overflowingly filled. I decided I ought to carry some buckets myself. Mario's wife was in the barn washing out a couple of huge glass jars surrounded by wicker baskets. In Italy, she observed, *la donna* did all the important jobs.

Pausing to learn that I am father of two daughters, she happily returned to her toil. We poured my buckets of juice into one of the jars. She had put little tiles over the holes at the top of the casks. Already a thick red substance was bubbling up underneath these and dripping down the sides of the barrels, for even now the wine was starting to ferment. Many casks, she said, would be empty this year. Too much rain in May and June had prevented any chance of a bumper crop.

'Next year the wine will be dearer,' she said. I asked how soon it took for the juice to ferment. 'By Christmas, more or less, it will be wine.'

Back by the wine-press Mario and Pepe dipped their glasses in the buckets, generously motioning to Jane, Tommy and me to do the same. Pepe pulled a hunk off a piece of bread, poured grape juice over it and handed it to me. Wasps hovered around the teeming liquid as it oozed from the press.

As the red juice poured out, one of the ancient ladies hobbled down the steps, sat on a plastic wine crate beside us all and put on her spectacles to watch. Still she addressed not a word to anyone. I attempted a second conversation with her, but Mario, resting for a couple of moments on an old bedstead, explained that he had grown so exasperated with their crazed old ways that he had built for them a completely new house in a perfectly traditional Umbrian style, twenty metres from his own home. Thus he escaped their chattering. Now they were so deaf that they never spoke a word.

Mario urged me to take a walk up the hillside to the church of San Fortunato. He told me there might be poisonous snakes in the olive trees. Jane Andersen added that the Bocciani family always kept an antidote in their refrigerator. 'You take up to twenty minutes to die from a snake bite,' she comforted me, 'so if you call out in pain, we'll find you in time.' Reassured, I strolled without anxiety past a garden of vegetables and peppers, and up past vines already lined with cow dung. Red and black, yellow and white butterflies fluttered around. The sun beat down. Suddenly I heard the screech of the caterpillar tracks of a tractor, and looked down to see that Pepe had abandoned wine-making and was ploughing the hard soil.

San Fortunato's church was locked, but the modern chalets and cultural centre surrounding it were bursting with life. A group of eager postulants sat around their guru, meditating on heaven-knows-what religious notions.

By the time I got back to the farm the vintage had been pressed. The women were washing the equipment and putting it back into the cellar to wait until next year. Since everyone was busy except me and I could not find Jane and Tommy, I sat in the car with my legs dangling outside and gazed across the valley, now entirely cleared of mist and entrancingly green – a special green sheen which the Umbrians rightly claim can be found nowhere else in Italy. I could see as far as Perugia, to the little industrial town of Ponte San Giovanni and to Bastia, though the haze now made it difficult to discern its medieval heart. Olive groves and meadows, vineyards and clumps of trees alongside a few ploughed fields vied with clouds of smoke where farmers were burning the stubble. A cross rose from the top of a far-off hill.

Mario finished sweeping out the barn and came over to talk to me. He asked how old I was and told me that he was sixty-five. From his looks I could scarcely believe it, but he went on to describe his war service as a partisan.

Then, as I love to do, we spoke about wine and food. Most people laud above all the flesh and Chianti of Tuscany. Said Mario: 'Tuscany and Umbria are the same – the greatest regions in Italy for meat and wine, though our wine is better than theirs.' He swiftly added what seemed to me a generous concession to Tuscan vintages, 'Even so, ours get better as you near the Tuscan border.' As for meats, he cautioned me, 'The best beasts these days go to Brazil. Don't expect these days ever to eat the old Perugian lamb or beef,' he lamented. 'Yet we still have superb oil and splendid grain.' A further sad tale was the story of the flight of young people from the land. 'They no longer can do what my generation and my ancestors have always done.' Mario pinched three black-red fingers as he enumerated these gifts: raising cattle, cultivating vines, harvesting. Young people, he observed, want instant cash and instant cash comes from offices and factories, not from farms.

Then he cheered up. 'Have you explored the farm?' he asked, as a prelude to taking me on a tour of his property. Mario pulled off his shirt and dumped it in a concrete vat of

4

water against an outside wall. We walked through a plot of dahlias and past a row of potted flowers. The heat of the sun bounced off the ochre walls of the farm buildings. Below the pale pink pantile roofs were smartly painted brown shutters and, below these, flaking red paint-covered double doors leading into byres.

Mario took me into the one housing four black and white cows and two bull calves. I asked what they were called, and he (no doubt momentarily taking me for an idiot) replied, '*mucce*' (that is, 'cows'), so I rephrased my question and asked their names. One he called 'la Cornetta' because of its curiously-shaped horns; the second he called 'Stellina', since its mother had been called 'Stella'; the third he called 'Mora', I think because she was all black; and the last he called 'la Piccola' because she had been tiny when born.

The women were now busy cooking, talking continually to each other in stentorian voices that could be heard wherever we walked. Mario gave me a flask of grape juice and led me into the house to watch television. That day Pope John Paul II was celebrating Mass in the presence of thousands in a sports stadium at Strasbourg, and the ceremony was, inevitably, being shown on Italian television.

I had already perceived that this was a devout household, for not one but two shrines of the Madonna had been created in the courtyard of the farm, each one lit by a bulb and adorned by rosary beads and flowers. Pepe wore a crucifix on a chain around his neck. In addition a portrait of St Francis amiably blessed the four cows and two bull calves. Inside the dining-room of the house – which was above the main cow-shed – no fewer than five pictures of Popes decorated the walls, including John XXIII, Paul VI and of course John Paul II himself. John XXIII, Mario told me, was a true and admirable Christian, 'for regarding all men as equal'. Over the wood fire – already lit, despite the delicious heat of the day – hung a copy of Leonardo da Vinci's 'Last Supper', its frame made of shells. Nearby was a sepia-tint of the crucifixion of Jesus.

5

In consequence I supposed that most of the household would be interested in watching at least part of the papal Mass. In fact the womenfolk bustled in and out of the room totally ignoring the televised and (as I judged, listening to his sermon) fascinating Vicar of Christ. Red-moustachioed Pepe, having returned from the field, was sunk in a deep sleep on a sofa by the fire. Jane and Tommy had temporarily disappeared again. That morning I alone (Mary in a household of Marthas) watched and worshipped with the supreme pontiff.

The Boccianis' refrigerator was in their living-room, which was separated from the kitchen by their dining-room, in which I worshipped and Pepe slept. In consequence his sleep was miserably interrupted, and my worship not at all disturbed, by the megaphone voices of Pepe's wife Elsa and her mother-in-law as they amicably shouted to each other while one tended the cooker and the other gathered provisions from the fridge.

Suddenly this noise was overtopped by the fearsome cacophany of a three-wheeled vehicle driven by four overwhelmingly vital teenaged boys, the sons of Elsa and their cousins. They stormed into the house with freshly caught fish, some still flapping with life. These last were held by the tail and bashed over the head several times to put them out of their misery. The children shouted aloud with excitement. Elsa was in ecstasy. The look of pleasure, as a mother exults in the exuberance of her sons and their young friends, beamed from her face as she shook her head at their antics, smiling at me with complicitous pleasure, a look which said, 'You too know what it is to have wickedly entrancing children.'

Then the meal began. We started with *penne al ragù*, spaghetti enriched with a meat sauce made from *budello*, which means entrails. The noise was tremendous. One child knocked a glassful of Coca-Cola over another's trousers. 'It's all right,' smiled the victim. 'I put on my dirty trousers to come out here this morning.'

The unruliness of the children matched the wildness of the conversation of Pepe and Mario, who were seated at either end of the long table and shouted continually to each other. From time to time both courteously brought me into the conversation, inviting me to express my halting views on Italian politics; spotting that I am a religious man and therefore asking whether the Church of England was really Catholic (as some had recently hinted); questioning me about the quality of French wine; begging me to explain to them the origin of the stunning accuracy of my Italian accent (my elder daughter has an Italian godmother).

The tablecloth, as one hardly needs say, was spotless. We all had napkins and cutlery, though Mario and Pepe blithely ignored these, eating with their fingers. Mario urged me to do the same, and for a while I did. For this he was reproved by his wife, beside whom I was seated, her face streaked with flour from wiping off the sweat as she cooked. So I dutifully obeyed the strongest person in the room and picked up my knife and fork again.

She and Elsa were rarely seated at the table, for they saw it as their duty to leap up and look after everyone's needs. As soon as the *penne al ragù* had been eaten, both women walked around the table carrying platters and handing out to each of us a piece of veal. Before I could start eating this, Elsa was behind me again, forking on to my plate a baked rice cake. Next came a succulent piece of pork, with slices of bread and salad.

I asked whether all these treats were their own produce, since I had observed their own pigs in a sty. By error (possibly due to the fact that the table creaked under the weight of not only the Boccianis' grape juice but also their wine, which Mario assiduously poured into my glass), for 'pig' I used the word *porcello* and not the usual word *maiale*. The children screamed with laughter. The menfolk, however, indulged in a raucously magical conversation about my own apparent knowledge of Italian *patois*, for *porcello* turns out to be acceptable for pig. In Foligno, I learnt, they use even more curious dialect words: not *il pane* for bread, for instance, but *le pene*.

White wine appeared on the table, alongside the grape juice, the red wine, the water, and Coca-Cola for the children. Mario now decided that water was the drink for him – though, as he explained to me, in the old days when he used to plough his fields with oxen, wine was his personal petrol.

Finally the women leapt once more to their feet and produced *dolce*, a superb fruit-cake, of two kinds from the refrigerator. To a slice of this cake they spooned on to our plates a bitter-sweet mixture of custard and chocolate. I asked Mario's wife what it was called. 'I don't know its name,' she replied. 'We eat it two or three times a year.'

As we drank little cups of black coffee and Mario and I vigorously plied our toothpicks, she said, 'When you are next in Italy, come here again.'

Assisi: pagan, Christian and gastronomic

On the way into Assisi from the Bocciani farm the road winds downhill and, reaching the plain, passes by a remarkably powerful church for such a rural setting: Santa Maria degli Angeli. This grandiose basilica, with its pompous, Roman-baroque marble façade, boasts three naves topped by a splendid Renaissance dome. Apart from the façade, the church was designed in the mid-sixteenth century by a Perugian architect named Gian Galeazzo Alessi. In Italy one is used to seeing great churches in the most unlikely places, but it still seems odd to find such a flamboyant building apparently serving a parish that can number no more than around 4,000 souls.

Of course it isn't a parish church at all. Here, nearly 800 years ago, the Franciscan order began. It started with a group of men that could be numbered on the fingers of both hands. Within a decade the order included 5,000 men, and a sister order had been founded to include the women who longed to follow the example of an Umbrian saint who was poor, frail and entirely open to the most difficult commands of the Christian gospel.

9

This is where these thousands first met together, squatting in the woods around what was then only a tiny chapel. The huge basilica which we see today was built to Alessi's plans three and a half centuries later, between 1569 and 1578. In the 1830s an earthquake left standing only the walls and the dome. The nineteenth-century Umbrians managed to rebuild the ruins by 1840, remaining faithful to the original designs, restoring the superb baroque apse. Only in 1927 did the architect Cesare Bazzanti add his near-megalomaniacal new façade, over whose apex a sculptor named Guglielmo Colosanti placed a huge gilded statue of Our Lady.

The church of Santa Maria degli Angeli is a kind of gigantic egg box protecting one precious and fragile egg. Under the dome is a much earlier, tiny church. Guide books will tell you that its origins go back as far as the fourth century, when a little chapel was built here by Syrian monks, and that the great founder of Western monasticism, St Benedict of Norcia, restored it two centuries later. Scholars have corrected this romantic legend (invented by a seventeenth-century Umbrian saint named Vitale) and have proved that this little chapel was built in the tenth century at the earliest, and probably in the eleventh.

So delicate is this chapel that it soon became known as 'the little plot', the 'Porziuncola'. Reports that the Virgin Mary had made appearances near this spot gave the chapel a new name: Santa Maria della Porziuncola. For two centuries Benedictine monks living on Mount Subasio used it as an adjunct, a kind of hermitage, to their abbey. Late in the twelfth century they abandoned the little chapel and it fell into ruin.

In 1207 it was restored by a young man who was to become Umbria's most famous saint and possibly the most celebrated saint in the world. Born in Assisi in 1182, St Francis was baptized John, but his wealthy father, the textile merchant Pietro di Bernardone, called him Francis. Francis's mother Pica came from troubadour country in France, and the boy grew up learning his native Umbrian,

Latin and French. He became a soldier, living life to the full, helped in his self-indulgent existence by Pietro's huge fortune.

Two setbacks to this hedonistic life forced him to think afresh the meaning and purpose of his own life. The Umbrian cities of Assisi and Perugia were continually at odds with each other, and as a result of one of these feuds Francis spent part of the years 1202 and 1203 in prison. Next he became seriously ill, and the severity of his illness gave him deep pause for thought. Still a soldier, he was at Spoleto planning an attack on Apulia when he had a disturbing vision of a hall hung with weapons of war.

The lavish gaiety of his former life soon failed to satisfy him. He still loved parties followed by riotous singing in the streets, but one night a fellow-reveller noticed that Francis was looking utterly dejected. 'What is upsetting you?' the friend jocularly asked. 'Have you taken a wife?' Francis replied, 'Yes, the fairest of all brides, Lady Poverty.'

Now he took to praying in the ruined chapel of the Porziuncola. One day he heard a voice from a crucifix: 'Francis, go and repair my house, which you see is now close to ruin.' In 1207 the chapel of the Porziuncola became the third ruined church restored by St Francis of Assisi. The Benedictines of Mount Subasio wished to give him the chapel but, true to his newly discovered love of poverty, Francis refused the gift. Instead he persuaded them to retain possession of the Porziuncola in exchange for an annual rent of a basket of fish.

Such behaviour scarcely endeared him to his father, especially as the saint had been using Pietro's fortune, unasked, to restore the ruined churches. Pietro angrily summoned his son to appear before the bishop, where the saint took off all his clothing and gave it back to his father. The bishop wrapped a cloak around the naked young man and Francis's dedication was complete. Dressed in rags, he made a pilgrimage to Rome. Meeting a leper there, he not only gave the man money but kissed his hideously diseased hand.

Such a man was now attracting a different kind of follower than the carefree young hedonists of Assisi. They made the Porziuncola their house of prayer, living in the surrounding woods in simple hermitages made of woven branches. By 1209 Francis had composed a rule of life for them, based on Jesus's instructions to his followers to 'take neither gold nor silver, nor copper in your belts', a rule of life which the saint persuaded Pope Innocent III to authorize. Three years later, in the little chapel, Francis vested a young girl named Clare as a nun. Equally dedicated to absolute poverty, St Clare became foundress of the order of Poor Clares.

In renouncing wealth and his former life, St Francis of Assisi did not renounce the love of singing which he had inherited from his mother, the daughter of French troubadours. Seventy years after his death his followers still recalled that 'Drunk with the love and compassion of Christ, the blessed Francis would sometimes sing in the French tongue the most sweet melodies that welled up inside him.' Since he no longer possessed any musical instrument, Francis would pick up a couple of sticks from the ground and pretend that one was a bow and the other a viol, mimicking playing it as he sang. But he also composed in Italian, and to this Umbrian saint we owe the first ever poem in the Italian language, the 'Canticle of the Creatures'. Abjuring earthly goods, Francis revelled in this poem in the gifts of God – 'brother Sun', 'sister Moon', 'brother Wind', 'sister Water' and 'mother Earth' with her plants and flowers.

As October 1226 approached Francis, already blind, knew that he was dying. Close to the Porziuncola he had designated a little cell as an infirmary. There he directed his fellow-monks to lay him in the dust. Today the cell is known as the chapel of the transition, the spot where St Francis passed to heaven. As he lay dying he added a new verse to his 'Canticle of the Creatures':

> Praise to you, my Lord, for our sister Death,
> for no one living can escape her.

> Alas for those who die in mortal sin!
> Happy are those whom she finds following your holy will,
>   for a second death will not harm them.

Then he told his followers never to leave that holy spot. 'Regard this place as the house of God, worthy of honour. Here sing to the Lord from the depth of your hearts and with your voices full of joy and praise.' On 3 October Francis of Assisi died. Fewer than two years later Pope Gregory IX declared him a saint.

More than seven and a half centuries later I can think of few other places than the Porziuncola where one can better savour the authentic flavour of St Francis. Over the entrance to the tiny chapel is a fresco by the nineteenth-century German artist Friedrich Overbeck, a Lutheran who had been converted to Catholicism under the inspiration of St Francis. He founded a school of artists known as the Nazarenes, who self-consciously devoted themselves to reviving the Umbrian style of painting. This fresco of 1829 detracts less from the simplicity of the little Romanesque chapel than does a foolishly ornate Gothic pinnacle on the pediment over the entrance. I wish the Franciscan custodians of this church would remove the pinnacle, but I suppose they dare not, since it contains a thirteenth-century statue of the Madonna.

Inside, scarcely anything has changed since Francis restored the church long ago. The stone walls are simple and unpolished, rough-hewn from Mount Subasio. In 1393 a monk called Ilaria came from Viterbo to paint the polyptych behind the altar, which depicts scenes from the life of St Francis flanking the annunciation of the Virgin Mary, to whom this little chapel is dedicated.

The infirmary where the 44-year-old Francis died stands on the right-hand side of the apse of Santa Maria degli Angeli. You enter it by the very door through which the saint was carried in 1226. On the outside wall is a maudlin fresco of 1886 by the Perugian artist Domenico Bruschi depicting the saint's death and burial. The walls inside carry sixteenth-

13

century frescos of Francis and his brethren by Giovanni di Pietro, who was known as Spagna, and over the altar is a superb ceramic of the saint by Andrea Della Robbia, made three and a half centuries after his death, his features extraordinarily expressive of both joy and asceticism. The cincture displayed here is said to be one worn by Francis himself.

There is much else to see, but nothing quite so evocative of Franciscan simplicity as these two chapels. The crypt of the huge basilica has been partly excavated to reveal traces of the earliest Franciscan convent constructed around the Porziuncola. Here is another masterpiece by Andrea Della Robbia, a blue and white ceramic which includes (as well as scenes of the nativity of Jesus, St Jerome in his cave and the coronation of the Virgin Mary) Della Robbia's version of St Francis receiving the stigmata. This refers to the tradition that two years before his death the saint was so ardently meditating on Mount La Verna about the crucified Jesus that the very wounds in Christ's hands, feet and side also marked Francis.

Did this really happen? The oldest known painting of the saint, a fresco in the chapel of St Gregory of the Sacro Speco, Subiaco, which describes him not as saint but as *frater*, depicts him without the stigmata. None the less, tradition insists that Francis was the very first of those few ardent followers of Jesus to be granted stigmatization. St Bonaventure, superior-general of the Franciscans, writing in the thirteenth century and describing how Francis lay dying, says that the humble saint gazed steadfastly into heaven 'without forgetting to cover the gash in his right side so that it could not be seen'.

Much else here serves as a reminder of the Umbrian who became one of the great saintly legends of Christendom. To the south of the chapel of the transition a corridor leads to the basilica's rose garden. On the way you pass a statue of Francis with a pair of doves. Francis, the lover of animals, appears again in the rose garden stroking his favourite ewe, sculpted by Vincenzo Rosignoli in 1912. St Bonaventure tells us that Francis was given a ewe while he lived at the Porziuncola. Deeply admiring the animal's simplicity, the saint taught it not to interrupt the prayers of the monks with too much bleating.

The rose garden certainly is remarkable, if not miraculous, because the roses have no thorns and when they bloom each spring they are streaked blood-red. Why? St Francis, we are told, was once so tempted to sin that he stripped himself naked and flung himself into a thorny bush to keep his flesh under control. The bush transformed itself into a thornless rose tree. Just beyond the rose garden St Bonaventure had a chapel constructed on the site at Santa Maria degli Angeli where St Francis was known to have had his cell. Here one of the frescos painted in the early sixteenth century by Tiberio d'Assisi charmingly depicts the saint in this thorny bush.

The saint, it must be added, was apparently skilled at coping with this kind of pain when tempted by the flesh. When he went east to try to convert the Sultan al-Malik al-Kamil to Christianity, a beautiful Egyptian whore invited him to bed. Francis agreed, took her to his room, lay in the fire and invited her to take off her clothes and join him. The woman was so astounded, especially when the flames failed to scorch the saint, that she abandoned her wanton life and became a Christian.

In the grotto underneath the chapel outside Assisi rest two huge ancient logs. They are said once to have supported the pulpit from which St Francis in 1216 proclaimed that Pope Honorius III, on a visit to Perugia, had granted the saint the so-called 'Porziuncola Pardon', a plenary indulgence granted to anyone who made a pilgrimage to this spot on 2 August.

Here is the explanation of why this humble home of humble monks should have been transformed into the great basilica of Santa Maria degli Angeli with its vast proportions and huge square. Scholars might doubt whether any such indulgence was granted by Honorius III and announced by St Francis, especially since this pardon seems to have been

15

ignored for at least fifty years after the saint's death; but soon crowds of men and women thronged the holy spot where he lived and died, convinced that here they could find forgiveness for their sins. The basilica was built to accommodate them all.

Before leaving do not fail to visit the museum in the Antico Convento, if only to pause before two masterpieces. The first is a portrait of Francis, attributed to Cimabue. This time the marks of the crucified Jesus are clearly visible on the saint's hands and feet. His face bears that expression of sweet melancholy which we have already seen in Andrea Della Robbia's terracotta.

The second masterpiece is a crucifix, painted in the first half of the thirteenth century by Giunta Pisano. Already we see the spiritual influence of Francis himself affecting the art of a Pisan master. Although the style of the crucifix remains medieval, a new passion is appearing. No longer is Jesus a hierarchical figure, with the cross a throne from which he reigns. Instead we gaze on the intensely human Jesus whom Francis so fervently worshipped, twisted in pain and half-naked. The suffering Christ has entered the iconography of Western art.

St Francis was not buried where he died but in the church of San Giorgio, Assisi. The day after his canonization Pope Gregory IX laid the cornerstone of what we now call the lower church of San Francesco, which the Pope conceived as a fitting resting-place for the relics of this revered poor one, or *poverello*.

Santa Maria degli Angeli is nearly four and a half kilometres south-west of Assisi, and as you drive up to the city the massive substructure of the basilica of San Francesco rises above you. The city rises up to 500 metres above sea-level, but is beautifully sheltered from harsh winds by Mount Subasio, whose highest peak reaches 1,290 metres. On the way to the Porta San Francesco try to counteract the baleful effect of countless tourist shops offering cheap trinkets by pausing at the ancient gateway of San Pietro and relishing the Romanesque-Gothic abbey church dedicated to the same saint.

The spirit of St Francis has deeply affected the people of Assisi, as I know from personal experience. The first time I ever drove up into the city my ramshackle car began to hiss steam from its radiator as we passed through the Porta San Francesco and began to climb the hill. Switching off the engine, I alighted in moderate despair only to discover four men already willing to push me and my family to the top of the hill, after which one of them kindly ran in front of us, leading us to a Fiat garage as we rolled slowly downhill.

Such is the all-pervasive memory of St Francis that it comes as a surprise in Assisi to drive to the Piazza del Commune and find yourself at the heart of what was once an Etruscan and then a Roman *municipium*. As well as the remains of Roman walls, the most impressive Roman sight is the so-called Temple of Minerva on the north-east side of the piazza, a temple whose pediment is borne on Corinthian columns almost certainly erected in the first century BC. Only in the sixteenth century was it converted into the Christian church of Santa Maria sopra Minerva, to be re-dedicated a century later to St Philip Neri and incongruously re-modelled inside in the baroque style by Giacomo Giorgetti. Before its uneasy transformation it served as the people's assembly hall. The exterior remains happily unspoilt and imposingly Augustan.

This square stands virtually on the site of the old Roman forum. A museum of Etruscan and Roman finds is situated close by in the crypt of the now demolished medieval church of San Nicolò, in whose place stands the city post office, designed by Ruggiero Antonelli in 1927 – one of the few modern buildings in this whole pink and white city. From the crypt you walk underground into the excavations of the forum itself. The poet Sextus Propertius was born at Assisi, and it is entrancing to find in the museum several inscriptions referring to his family, as well as statues of Castor and Pollux.

17

Next to the post office stands Assisi's fourteenth-century town hall, the Palazzo Communale, once called the Palazzo dei Priori. Now the municipal museum as well as the seat of government, it really consists of no fewer than four blocks of buildings, their medieval irregularity adding charm to the whole piazza.

The seductiveness of the Piazza del Commune itself is enhanced by its own irregularity and by the elegant fountain situated at its wider end (Assisi was famous for its springs as far back as Roman times). Rarely quiet, it boasts cafés, restaurants and elegant shops. Each morning, except on Sundays, a market spreads out from the piazza into the Piazzeta del'Erbe. Sometimes a wedding party emerges from the town hall, everyone smiling, chattering wildly and carrying flowers. The pigeons of the piazza are fed here daily at noon, and in my experience it is wise to stand well upwind of them.

Alongside the Temple of Minerva rises the slender battlemented tower of the Palazzo del Capitano del Popolo, built between 1212 and 1305 and separating the temple from the thirteenth-century palace itself, also battlemented, also built of warm white stone. At the foot of this tower look out for three narrow bricks set into the wall. They constitute a fascinating relic of medieval affairs in Assisi. Set here in 1349, these bricks indicate exactly the proper size of a medieval brick or tile – *pianella* (a roofing tile), *mattone* (a baked hollow brick) and *quadrello* (a square tile) to use their proper terms. Underneath them is set a strip of metal 104 centimetres long, Assisi's medieval equivalent of a metre. Next to it is the measure for a foot, used to measure a *pede di legno* or a foot of wood. You can trace gaps where other such measures have either fallen out or been stolen.

From this square let me suggest a walk around Assisi which takes in entrancing parts of the city that are off the beaten tourist track, in addition to the well-known masterpieces which no one should miss. Via San Paolo runs from the Palazzo del Capitano del Popolo alongside the Sala di

Minerva, which clearly incorporates part of a Roman wall and is today used to house entertaining exhibitions of Assisi's past. I once saw displayed there some early thirteenth-century scissors, used for cutting the hair of nuns, alongside some medieval children's walking chairs and chamber pots. Another exhibition of implements of the countryside boasted savage wolf- and bird-traps.

Walk along the Via San Paolo, so named because no. 5 is a tiny thirteenth-century church, dedicated to St Paul. Dono Doni frescoed the three saints over the entrance in the second half of the sixteenth century. On the right of the street, notice how the Roman wall is topped by the stones of the medieval one, and admire too the tall, elegant arch over the door of no. 18. Then turn left down the Vicolo San Stefano. Here, on a clear day, you can sit and see not only Santa Maria degli Angeli but also in the distance Perugia, some twenty-six kilometres away.

Continue down the *vicolo* to find the church of San Stefano to the left, one of the oldest in Assisi, dating back as far as the twelfth century. Its façade is polite, simple and moving. Inside, under a Gothic roof, are the remains of fourteenth- and fifteenth-century frescos. Although the church seems to be in a backwater, with the press of Assisi's tourists suddenly absent, people will be here, meditating and praying. The font was once a millstone. On the right is a modern confessional, one of the few pieces of twentieth-century metalwork of which I entirely approve. As for San Stefano's bell-tower, the people of Assisi dub it 'the sail'. When St Francis died, they tell you, its bells tolled spontaneously, even though, as they immediately add, the tower was not built until a few years later.

Rosemary and a fig tree overhang the wall of a neighbouring house. The *vicolo* still descends, and at the end you turn left down more steps by way of the Piazzetta Verdi, through a haphazard arch to reach a confraternity ahead decorated with the seven spiritual works of mercy. Alas, with time these have decayed, since they were done in tempera, not

19

frescoed, but maybe one can still make out the converted sinner, the ignorant under instruction, the doubtful counselled, the sorrowful being comforted, wrongs patiently borne, injuries forgiven, and prayers being offered for both the living and the dead.

Turn left now up the Via Eugenio Brizi, past a restaurant piquantly and devoutly named 'Buca di San Francesco'. This is a street of clothes and silver shops. On the left as you enter Piazza Giuseppe Sbarglini is a grisly named curiosity: a doorway of death. The actual doorway was blocked up in the late thirteenth century, though its contours can readily be made out, and it is surmounted by a cross made of iron. Invariably such doorways of death (which you find in Gubbio too) front staircases, but when trade flourished in medieval Assisi, the workshop doors next to them became far more important. The many warring factions in the town meant that every house needed defending, and it was easier to defend one entrance rather than two. On the other hand, from time to time the staircase doorways needed opening up again, to let out the corpse of one who had died upstairs. Filled in again after the funeral, these doorways of death were adorned with the Christian symbol of hope in the resurrection of us all. Yet they make me shudder, just as I invariably do in Umbria when I see in a cake shop those delicious sweets which are called *le fave morti* and which were, in the past, bought from nunneries for funerals and for All Souls' Day. (These days the Umbrians eat them all year round.)

From Via Eugenio Brizi turn right into Via Bernardo da Quintavalle, named after the man who offered hospitality to St Francis at the beginning of the saint's new life. Over his house a plaque in Latin reads: 'Here Blessed Bernardo da Quintavalle received St Francis for dinner and offered him a bed for the night, and here he saw him in ecstasy.' This little-known house really marks the beginning of the Franciscan order, for Francis had been considering only the course of his own future life until Bernardo da Quintavalle declared his wish to follow the saint.

As you walk along, a glance to either side of the *via* offers treats. Look left up Vicolo Rocchi to glimpse the tower of the Piazza del Commune. Then to the right appears the smallest street in Assisi, more like a medieval tunnel than a street. Soon after on the right comes the entrance to the Piazza Vescovado. The eleventh-century church of Santa Maria Maggiore in this piazza was once the cathedral of Assisi. Its sweet rose window is inscribed with the date 1163 and the name of the man who built it, Giovanni da Gubbio. The campanile is part-Romanesque, part-Gothic in style. Under this church is a frescoed Roman house, not yet open to the public unless you can pose as a specialist scholar and thus be allowed entry. And in the square stands the episcopal palace in which St Francis stripped and gave back his clothing to his father. At the opposite corner of the piazza rises the square tower of the church of the nunnery of San Giuseppe, whose order, with the support of the Bishop of Assisi, hid many Jews during World War II.

From here, leaning against a wall, you can look across to the church dedicated to the foundress of the Poor Clares, Santa Chiara. It seems to have been built of superimposed sandwiches of white bread, honey and jam. Its rose window, built almost exactly a century after that of Santa Maria Maggiore, is of the most exquisite Gothic. Colossal flying buttresses, round-arched, support the side walls of the church.

From the corner of Piazza Vescovado walk up Via San Agnese, which is named after St Clare's sister. This way, leading past an olive grove, reaches the arches of the huge convent (where today are cloistered some fifty or sixty Poor Clares) and the Piazza Santa Chiara, a balcony overlooking a great swathe of Umbrian plain.

In the mid-thirteenth century Filippo da Campello designed the basilica of Santa Chiara to honour St Francis's first woman disciple. Clare was a girl of spirit, and had already twice turned down suitors before she met Francis at the age of eighteen. Her rich and noble parents, Favarone di

Offreduccio and Ortolana Fiumi, pleaded with her not to renounce the world, but she took up secret refuge with some Benedictine nuns at Bastia to avoid their anger. There her sister Agnese joined Clare, and after her father's death the mother too joined the daughters.

These three were the cell from which grew the order of the Poor Clares. Under the guidance of St Francis, who drew up a rule for them, they moved to the church of St Damiano just outside Assisi, the same church where Francis had heard a voice from the crucifix urging him to rebuild the ruined house of God. Clare wanted her sisters to live not simply without personal property, but without communal property too. In the higher realms of the Church few thought such a decision prudent, but she managed to persuade Pope Innocent III to grant her what she called this 'privilege'. Even so, the Church authorities frequently tried to take away the privilege, though invariably Clare's determination routed them. Yet she was no harsh woman. At night she toured her convent making sure that the nuns' bedclothes were properly tucked in. One of her letters is extant, reminding the superior of another convent of Poor Clares that since 'our bodies are not made of brass' too much austerity is foolish.

This splendid woman was herself often seriously ill, but she remained superior of the Poor Clares for forty years, until her death in 1253. Her canonization was as swift as that of St Francis, for two years later Pope Innocent IV declared her a saint. Two years after that work began on her basilica in Assisi. In 1265 it was consecrated. Today the flying buttresses on the south side are walled up, for behind them are hidden the convent, the cloister and the nunnery garden.

Lions guard the doorway of the church, which opens into a delicious Gothic nave, with a frescoed apse in which hangs a thirteenth-century crucifix by an unknown Umbrian artist. The transepts too are beautifully frescoed. And the chapel of the Blessed Sacrament in the basilica of Santa Chiara stands on the site of the church of San Giorgio, whose priests taught St Francis to read, and where his body lay until his own basilica was ready to receive his remains.

Next to this is a chapel containing one of the most remarkable crucifixes in Umbria. Painted on wood in the twelfth century, this is the crucifix which once hung in the church of San Damiano and spoke to St Francis. Artistically I find it fascinating to contrast it with, for example, the crucifix by Giunta Pisano which we have already seen in the museum of Santa Maria degli Angeli. Painted a century or so earlier, the crucifix from San Damiano is far more hieratic, far less tormented than that painted by Giunta under the influence of Franciscan devotion.

Do not miss in this basilica the entrancing painting of St Clare herself, which is so elongated, her fingers so slender and refined, that some have attributed it to Cimabue himself, though the more cautious prefer to declare it a work of the 'maestro di Santa Chiara'. On either side of the saint the artist has depicted scenes from her life with great vivacity and considerable wit.

At the bottom left-hand side Clare, with long blonde hair and wearing a rich red robe, is seen in Assisi cathedral on Palm Sunday receiving an olive branch from Bishop Guido. The bishop is privy to the plot, having already learnt from St Francis that Clare will flee that same night from her home and be clothed as a nun in the Porziuncola. In the next panel up, Francis and his followers meet Clare, along with her ladies-in-waiting, including her nurse, Bona di Guelfuccio. Here the 'maestro di Santa Chiara' has brilliantly contrasted the simplicity of the Franciscans with the bejewelled wealth of Clare and her retinue. The next panel up shows all this transformed. Clare's blonde hair has been shorn by Francis; her head is covered with a black veil; a simple tunic has replaced her red robe.

The next two panels expound the impotent rage of Clare's father. In the top one to the right he has arrived with his followers at the Benedictine nunnery of Bastia and attempts to seize his daughter, but she thwarts him by clinging to the altar and Offreduccio is forced to give up. When, however, his second daughter Agnes joins Clare, Offreduccio attempts to bring her home by force. Now Clare performs one of the jolliest miracles in Christian history. Her prayers make Agnes so heavy that none of Offreduccio's servants can lift her. When the enraged father raises his hand to strike Agnes, Clare paralyses it.

Beneath this scene a sixth panel depicts another of Clare's miracles. In the refectory of San Damiano, as she blesses bread before handing it to her nuns, each piece is miraculously embossed with a cross. The last two panels depict her final days on earth. Sustained by a group of heavenly virgins, all wearing crowns, she is covered with an exquisite pall by the Blessed Virgin herself. Finally, Pope Innocent IV censes the body of the dead saint, accompanied by bishops and Franciscans (though not, curiously enough, any of her Poor Clares). This same body you can venerate today in the crypt of the basilica, reached by a staircase in the centre of the nave, a crypt ineptly re-Gothicized in 1935.

By taking the steps leading back into the city from the Piazza Santa Chiara and then turning right up to the Vicolo Superiore di San Antonio, you reach the draper's shop where, perhaps, St Francis was born. His nephew Piccardo transformed it into an oratory, and over the Gothic doorway an inscription reads, '*Hoc oratorium fuit bovis et asini stabulum, in quo natus est B. Franciscus mundi speculum*' – 'This oratory, once a cattle-stall, was the birthplace of Francis, who reflected Jesus to the world.'

Vicolo Superiore di San Antonio winds on to reach Piazza Chiesa Nuova, where in 1615 Philip III of Spain decided to build a church on the supposed site of a house belonging to Francis's father. Possibly such a house did stand here, for Pietro derived his money from the cloth trade and a regular market used to be held on this spot. At any rate, the Spanish king built here the baroque Chiesa Nuova, and in 1984 the sculptor Roberto Joppolo created bronze statues of the saint's mother and father to adorn the piazza in which it stands, presiding over the open-air music and pageants which frequently take place here.

The rear of the Palazzo Communale backs on to this piazza, and you can walk back directly into the Piazza del Commune. High above it towers Assisi's splendid medieval fortress, the Rocca Maggiore. To reach it entails a stiff climb but no one should balk at it. Frederick Barbarossa built a fortress on this site in 1174, but the people of Assisi resented living under the tutelage of the Teutons and pulled it down a quarter of a century later. The present powerful building dates from 1357 and is largely the work of the papal legate Albornoz, though it was repeatedly extended during the next two centuries. Irregular and formidable, its keep offers some of the finest views in Umbria, with Spoleto rising to the south, Mount Subasio to the east and to the north the gash of the Tescio gorge. But before climbing up to the Rocca Maggiore, by now it is surely time to eat.

The Scalinata della Fortezza leads up from the Piazza del Commune to the restaurant La Fortezza, where you enter past part of the Roman wall which serves as an interior wall of the restaurant itself. My host when I ate there (who says I must not name him in the book, but simply thank the Azienda di Promozione Turistico of Assisi, for which he has the pleasure to work) suggested that since the father of the restaurateur was born in the Dolomites, we might that day renounce the excellent wines of Umbria and start with a white Trentino Pinot Grigio, Villa de Vardi DOC, from that region. I readily agreed, for the wine turned out to justify its description of *amàbile*, which in this case meant attractive, charming, a little bit sweet but sharpish too.

The food was Umbrian *per eccellenza*. Before the meal started my host asked if I would like pigeon. I realized why he asked at that moment, since the chef began preparing and cooking it only when it was ordered. He plucked the bones from the bird (this is not in fact the local custom, save in such succulent places) and covered it with a sauce made – as the restaurateur kindly explained – of extra virgin olive oil, rosemary, sage, anchovy, dry white wine and wine vinegar, the pigeon livers as a binding and heaven knows what else. The pigeons took forty-five minutes of delicate cooking.

Meanwhile we whetted our appetites with a mixture of seasoned tomatoes, mushrooms, gherkins, with *crostini* (pieces of fried, toasted bread) and *bruschetta* (garlic bread). Next we ate *vernaiola* (water melon), along with slices of toast bearing four sorts of pâté: salmon, chicken, ham and olive.

The pigeon itself was gently washed down with a red wine from the same region as the white, a Teroldino Rotalione. Umbrians love to *discutere* over a meal – a word meaning something between reason about matters, discuss questions, tell stories, offer opinions and debate. The noise was not as great as it had been over the family feast at the Bocciani farm, but it was equally instructive and joyful.

We talked of the first modern historian to tackle the problems raised by the life of St Francis. He turned out to be the French Huguenot Paul Sabatier. I asked about tourist access to and from Assisi. There are, I learnt, two regular excursions from here to Franciscan sites: one to La Verna (which happens to be just over the Tuscany border), where St Francis received the stigmata; and a second to such sites as Greccio, where he invented the Christmas crib in a most delightful fashion (as shall be explained later in this book). We spoke of regional cooking, and I discovered that quails cooked on a spit are in Umbria deemed to have been cooked 'Franciscan fashion'.

We ended our meal with a slice of pear and Parmesan cheese, a combination that few can tire of. As for the wine, the restaurateur had said '*è molto profumato*'. My host added, 'It is a traitor.' He was right. The Teroldino Rotalione betrayed me with its kiss. I cannot remember much else from that delightful afternoon.

On that visit to Umbria I was staying not in the city but at a splendid country 'hacienda' (*azienda* in Italian), Le Silve di Armenzano, set beautifully in the hills outside Assisi. Le Silve offers walking, horse-riding, tennis, a swimming pool and a sauna, all of which (save tennis) I am game for. But for the rest of that day I simply slept.

How, I wonder, do those 300,000 visitors cope who, on some days at the height of the tourist season, manage to spend no more than two hours in Assisi? A wiser group stays for three or more days (and in fact Assisi hosts what the trade calls 800,000 'overnights' each year). Even then one should return another year to sample everything again – plus a little more, including some of the city's festivals.

Assisi relishes its historic past, and not only that connected with the celebrated saint who has provided the city with a yearly round of religious festivals. Early in May, for instance, the Piazza del Commune and its surrounding streets are the setting for the Festa di Calendimaggio. This costume-bedecked spectacle re-creates the rivalry which existed between the upper and lower city from the fourteenth century till the mid-sixteenth. A festival queen, Madonna Primavera, is elected; the mayor of Assisi ceremoniously hands over his keys to the Master of the Field, the Maestro di Campo; minstrels, exquisitely dressed musicians, costumed men bearing banners, and a riot of colourfully clad women parade through the streets. On the final day of the festival a mock battle is re-enacted in the Piazza del Commune, with a panel of judges choosing the victors.

Assisi is crammed with other treasures as great as, and even greater than, the ones we have so far seen. The cathedral of San Rufino is one, dedicated to the patron saint of the city, a third-century missionary and martyr who met his death when the pagans threw him into the River Chiascio. His fellow-Christians built a small chapel on this spot to house his damp bones. They replaced it with a greater one in the eleventh century, which in turn was supplanted by the present Romanesque church which Giovanni di Gubbio began building in 1140. Pope Gregory IX consecrated the new altar in 1228 and twenty-five years later Pope Innocent IV consecrated the whole church.

The campanile derives from all three churches, set on Roman foundations, rising on eleventh-century stones (in

which the church clock is set) and rising above the clock in
a severely elegant Romanesque style that mirrors the sparely
beautiful façade of Giovanni's church. Giovanni wanted this
façade to presage the three naves of his interior, so he
crowned his three doorways with three rose windows, the
middle ones being the greatest in the case of windows and
doors alike. In between the doorways runs a delicate row of
columns whose purpose, so far as I can tell, is entirely
decorative.

The twelfth-century churchman and woman loved symbolism; their architects relished supplying it. Around the
central rose window Giovanni set the symbols of the four
evangelists: the winged lion of St Mark, the angel of St
Matthew, the winged bull of St Luke and the eagle of St John.
As for the lions flanking the main doorway, it requires some
historical ingenuity to decipher their symbolic meaning.
The one who looks left represents Jesus abolishing pagan
sacrifices; the other one the Jewish notion of sacrificing a
scapegoat.

I sometimes think one should simply admire the Romanesque beauty of all this without troubling too much about
what everything stands for. Certainly the interlaced patterns
around the three doors are at once aesthetically calm and
complex. But symbolism aggressively fights its way out of
them. In the lunette of the central doorway Jesus sits
enthroned and crowned in glory. On his right the Madonna
holds the same Jesus as an infant. On his left St Rufino
preaches his gospel. But what of the sun and moon on either
side of the enthroned Christ's head? One represents darkness,
the other light, for Christ is Lord of both.

The carvings above the left doorway are partly mutilated
and less ornate than those in the lunette of the main doorway.
Yet these too spoke of theology and politics to medieval
minds. Take the medallion of the Lamb of God holding his
cross. He is flanked by two eagles, symbols of the Holy Roman
Empire, both subservient to Christ's rule.

Galeazzo Alessi, who created the church of Santa Maria

degli Angeli to house the Porziuncola in the sixteenth century, also transformed the interior of San Rufino. He worked here in the nick of time, since the twelfth-century church was about to collapse. He was acute enough to preserve some evocative memorials from the old church, such as the ancient font used at the baptism of St Francis, the third-century sarcophagus of St Rufino himself, and another exquisite, third-century sarcophagus which depicts the myth of Diana and Endymion.

Once Alessi had felt free to change the interior of a twelfth-century church, others followed suit. The baroque chapel of the Blessed Sacrament, for instance, was created by Giacomo Giorgetti in the seventeenth century and today houses paintings by the Genovese artist Giovanni Andrea Carlone which were executed two centuries earlier. Another unusual treasure for an Umbrian church is found in the chapel of the Madonna of Tears: a polychrome fifteenth-century *pietà* from Germany. Its name derives from the legend that in 1494 Mary wept over the viciousness of the internecine wars of Assisi. The Christ of this terracotta seems to me too unmistakably and starkly dead to have wept.

Polished cherubic heads hold up the arm-rests of the Renaissance choir stalls, which are by Giovanni da Sanseverino. Dono Doni created a 'Deposition' for the cathedral, and the nineteenth-century Parisian sculptor Paul Lemoyne supplied a statue of St Rufino in marble. In 1882 Giovanni Dupré sculpted a marble likeness of St Francis – thank heavens the very last of Dupré's sentimental works, though his daughter was at hand in 1888 to sculpt an equally cloying St Clare for her basilica.

Finally, seek a sacristan and pay a visit to the crypt of the cathedral, for here are preserved cool columns and arches from the eleventh-century Carolingian church on which the present basilica stands.

Make your way from the cathedral piazza down the medieval Via San Rufino to the Piazza del Commune and continue by way of the Via Portica, Via Seminario and Via San

Francesco to Assisi's showcase, the double basilica of San Francesco. Here, quite simply, one church has been piled on top of another, the two prosaically designated the lower basilica and the upper.

Although the lower church was not totally finished by 25 May 1230, on that day the bones of the saint were triumphantly carried from San Giorgio and interred there. Already Francis was famous, and for fear that his relics might be stolen, the site of the grave was kept secret – so secret that eventually its whereabouts were forgotten. Excavations in 1570, 1607 and 1806 failed to locate it. Only in 1818 were the saint's bones rediscovered. Today the tomb in the crypt of the lower church is open for the prayers of the faithful and the veneration of tourists, who alas frequently break the rule of silence in this sacred spot.

You reach this lower church, logically enough, by means of the lower courtyard of the Piazza di San Francesco, a courtyard flanked by shady colonnades whose pillars are contentedly crumbling with age. The entrance, though ornate enough, is shaded by an elegant white Romanesque campanile, a foretaste of the powerful Romanesque nave inside.

Five of the greatest artists of the thirteenth and fourteenth centuries decorated this church and the upper basilica. They were Cimabue, his pupil Giotto, the Lorenzetti brothers and Simone Martini. Cimabue was a Florentine whose real name was Cenni di Pepi. His nickname means ox-head. The soubriquet in no way seems to have dimmed his estimate of his own powers. Born in 1240, he was interred sixty years later with an epitaph asserting his supremacy in the field of painting:

> *Credidit ut Cimabos picturae castra tenere,*
> *Sic tenuit vovens: nunc tenet astra poli.*

(Cimabue was confident of holding the fort of picture-making, and held it according to his vow. Now he holds the stars of Heaven.)

And indeed in the late thirteenth century this man was the most celebrated and among the most talented painters in Europe.

Cimabue's work in the lower basilica includes a famous portrait of St Francis himself. You can find it in a group painted on the wall of the right transept which depicts the enthroned Madonna guarded by four angels and the *poverello* himself. Francis is standing to one side, tonsured, bearing the stigmata, his face again doleful in curious contrast with the very first rule of his Franciscans, which declares that the friars, far from being sad and gloomy, must display themselves as 'gay and pleasant and joyful in the Lord'.

I find it intriguing to compare Cimabue's portrait of the saint with that of Simone Martini, which is also in the lower basilica. Martini was in his mid-twenties when Cimabue died, and he came not from Florence but from Sienna. Like Cimabue, his work remains hieratic and Byzantine, but to this he added an expressiveness of gesture and glance that can still startle. His portrait of St Francis shows a man who combined with his graciousness a will of iron. His eyes are penetrating and sharp, even while one hand gracefully points to his heart and another cajoles his company to greater asceticism and devotion.

In 1320 two other Siennese masters, Pietro Lorenzetti and his brother Ambrogio, frescoed the left arm of the transept with luminous scenes from the passion of Jesus. But the supreme masterpieces here are undoubtedly those of Giotto. Dante's *Purgatory*, referring to Cimabue's claim to absolute supremacy as a painter, pointedly noted how Giotto had superseded him:

> *Oh vana gloria dell'umane posse!*
> *Com' poco verde in su la cima dura,*
> *se non è giunta dall'etati grosse!*
> *Credette Cimabue nelle pintura*
> *tener lo campo, e ora ha Giotto il grido,*
> *si che la fama di colui è oscura.*

(O powers of man! How vain your glory, nipped
Even in its greenest height, unless a less bright age
Should follow. Cimabue thought to laud it
In the realm of painting. Now the cry is Giotto's,
With Cimabue's name eclipsed.)

Later writers, elaborating on this, described how Cimabue discovered Giotto tending his father's sheep outside Florence and took the young man into his own studio, therefore nurturing the artist who was to outreach him in genius.

If Cimabue is striving to transform his medieval artistic inheritance (and thereby producing works of immense spiritual power), Giotto brings to Assisi a lightness of touch and a humanity which surpass any other paintings in the basilica. His nativity, with a donkey and a cow peering at the infant Jesus in his swaddling clothes, while shepherds look after several black sheep as well as white ones; his flight into Egypt, with the baby resolutely clinging to his mother as they ride the distinctively male donkey; the raising of Lazarus and the lovely 'Noli me tangere' in the chapel of the Magdalen – all these pulsate with human breath. Looking at these wonders I always find it hard to tear myself away and descend the flight of stairs in the middle of the nave in order to find the crypt and the sarcophagus which houses the bones of the saint who inspired them all.

The unknown architect who designed the upper basilica of San Francesco in the early thirteenth century seems, in retrospect, to have done so entirely for the sake of Giotto's frescos. In fact, he created a perfect space, bounded by pure Umbrian Gothic, and Cimabue and his school decorated the apse and transept with paintings of a disturbing vigour. Then Giotto added two Old Testament scenes, from the life of Isaac, which instantly bring peace, followed by the deeply moving 'Deposition' of Jesus. By this time he had begun reading Franciscan spiritual writings, and from the 1290s until the early fourteenth century he and his pupils produced in the upper basilica frescos unequalled in power, devoted to the life of the *poverello*.

The sequence begins over the high altar on the south wall. If I am to choose the two frescos which most affect me, they are that depicting St Francis giving back his clothing to his father and that showing the saint preaching to the birds. In the first, the bishop modestly turns away his face as he wraps a blue towel round Francis's loins and legs, while the saint's father is restrained from smacking his son's face only by a sturdy follower. In the second, the birds seem far more attentive than any congregation I have ever seen.

Everywhere, as you wander through this city, appear panoramas of the pine-studded *campagna*. The Lombards strengthened the Roman fortifications of Assisi by adding medieval walls. Once, in the Via Metastasio, in a bar which overlooked the walls and a vast stretch of green Umbrian countryside, I carried my own *vino tipico* and salami sandwich from the counter on to the terrace. The waiter rushed up to help me, at which I observed that I was merely imitating St Francis himself. 'I too,' he replied, adding, 'actually, I'm his cousin.'

Gazing over these ancient walls entices the tourist to leave Assisi for a while, since outside the city the countryside unfolds magical towns and villages, with their churches and palaces. Drive south out of Assisi by way of Santa Maria degli Angeli, turn south-east along the SS75 and look for the road on the right to Cannara. This partly industrialized town is graced with three fine churches. San Francesco pokes the thumb of its stumpy tower at the sky and treasures a valuable painting of the Madonna and a couple of saints by Nicolò Alunno. The thirteenth-century San Biaglo rejoices in its elegant façade. San Matteo, built in 1786, houses many paintings and frescos from earlier centuries. Adding to these riches, the town hall has a museum with Roman remains excavated from nearby Urvinum Hortense.

From Cannara drive south-west to Cappuccini and then take the road south-east to reach Bevagna. The Romans called it Mevagna, and you can see the remains of their theatre and amphitheatre, their temple and their mosaics.

Roman walls (surmounted by thirteenth-century additions) surround the city, and the citizens have long built their houses over them.

Piazza delle Libertà, Bevagna, is beautiful. And in the central Piazza Silvestri, a perfect medieval survival, is an elegant fountain (admittedly put there in 1889 but still redolent of the Middle Ages). On one side rises the church of San Michele with a Romanesque façade and a Romanesque campanile whose lights match the little ones on the façade. In the same square is the Palazzo dei Consoli, built in 1270, with an outside staircase sweeping up to its entrance. To make the town centre even more enticing, the main piazza of Bevagna also boasts the church of San Silvestro, built in 1195 by an architect named Binello and his friend Rodolfo. They were so entranced with their own work that they inscribed their names and the date 1195 on the exquisitely carved entrance. The inscription (underneath a sculpture of St Michael sticking his lance down a dragon's throat) reads:

RODOLFUS BINELLU[S] FECER[UNT] H[A]EC OPERA
[CHRISTUS] BENEDICAT ILLOS SEMPER: MICHAEL CUSTODIAT

(Rodolfo and Binello executed this work.
May Christ always bless them. May St Michael protect them.)

Even more rewarding, in my view, is Montefalco, seven kilometres south-east from Bevagna and soon visible on its hill as you drive up to it through the olive trees. The walls of Montefalco are intact, its gateway fortified, its streets pleasingly narrow. The town is crammed with Romanesque churches and medieval palaces. The central piazza is a dream – octagonal, indeed virtually circular. Montefalco's grey-walled Palazzo Communale has an arcade matched by another line of arcading to its right. The theatre in the piazza was built in the eighteenth century and proves the fact by its economical elegance.

Via Rhingiera Umbra leads from here down to the former church of San Francesco, now a charming museum of religious art (the Musea Pinocateca ex Chiesa di San

Francesco, open from 10.00 to 12.00 and 13.30 to 18.00, closing on Saturdays at 11.45). A bottle of red Montefalco wine which I had just bought in the piazza protruded from my bag as I entered. When the custodian saw it she sagely observed, 'It rains here enough to swell the grapes properly.' In the church the frescos by Gozzoli are superb, especially the scene in the apse where a pretty red-haired St Francis has the cloak put around his naked body. Francesco Melanzio's 'Madonna del Soccorso' depicts a little boy fearfully fleeing under Mary's robe from a black devil. A little further on the same scene is painted by Tiberio d'Assisi, only this time the devil is even more fearsome, winged and with a serpent round his waist, and he has hold of the child by the neck of his shirt.

The route from Montefalco winds north-east for eleven and a half kilometres to Foligno. Situated where the valleys of the Clitunno and Topino meet, Foligno is, alas, not unspoilt. You have to wander among unappealing modern buildings to pick out the gems. Seek and you will find, for the façade of the cathedral is a haughty Romanesque masterpiece. The symbols of the four evangelists are set around the main rose window. The façade is further decorated with two other rose windows, a fine mosaic of Christ in majesty, his glory shared by St Francis and St Messalina, and a simple row of Romanesque openings below. I wish I could explain why every rose window is regrettably blocked up inside. Foligno cathedral also boasts a secondary Romanesque façade, by none other than the same Binello and Rudolfo who created San Michele and San Silvestro at Bevagna.

Adjoining the cathedral is the fourteenth-century Palazzo delle Canoniche; a late fourteenth-century bridge of sighs connects the cathedral with the Palazzo Trinci; and nearby in the Piazza Communale is the ancient, tumbledown Palazzo del Podestà, flanked by a couple of other medieval palaces. The side portal of the cathedral is as beautiful as its main doorway, and here I love to run my hand down the wooden doors carved in the eighteenth century.

If you wander down the alleyways of Foligno you surprise

yourself by coming upon medieval houses, fine churches and ancient archways. There are three baroque *palazzi* (Ubaldi, Manci-Salvini and Barnabò). Santa Maria Infraportas is a stubby little Romanesque church whose simplicity is the basis of its charm. The Oratorio della Nunziatella has a sensitive 'Baptism of Jesus' by Perugino. Look more closely and you will see that Foligno has preserved the regular pattern of her old Roman streets.

Yet I still find it difficult to believe that this industrialized city was the birthplace of a renowned medieval mystic named Angela. She was born here in the mid-thirteenth century, married and lived a life of considerable debauchery until the age of forty. Converted by the Franciscans, her desire to become a nun was thwarted by the fact that her husband and children were still alive. Angela therefore prayed for their deaths, and God granted her prayer.

Her husband once dispensed with, she conceived herself as mystically married to the triune God. 'You hold me and I hold you,' she wrote. 'Now,' Angela declared, 'whether waking or sleeping I began to have a constant divine sweetness in my soul.' Once she experienced eight continuous days of ecstasy when she lay utterly still, unable to speak. She died in 1309 and was beatified in 1693.

Her mystical revelations have survived her, dictated to her confessor and published as *The Book of Divine Consolation*. What amazed Angela most was that the Christ who, in her belief, had created the world and held all things in existence, empowered this world to crucify him. 'He gave power to the sharp thorns to enter and most cruelly wound his divine and trembling head; he empowered the bonds and bitter cords to bind him fast unto the pillar and tie his hands together,' she marvelled. 'He gave unto the hard nails power to pierce and enter his tender feet.'

Foligno celebrates its past each year by mounting a tournament in which men on horseback tilt at lances. Ten knights, each in the colour of one of the ten wards of the city, ride headlong, trying to collect three rings on the end of their lances. Naturally the womenfolk of Foligno refuse to be outdone by their men, and attend dressed in ruffs and furs and lavish medieval costumes. Foligno's Giostra della Quintana takes place on the second Saturday and the second and third Sundays in September.

Drive back towards Assisi on the SS75 and you reach the walled and turreted city of Spello. Not a house here is out of place, though everything seems to have grown haphazardly. Cypress trees fill the gaps between the houses. Square machicolated towers jut here and there, with trees growing on top of some of them.

More than any other of the towns we have just visited, Spello has preserved its Roman remains and still uses them, especially three of its gates set in the medieval walls. In Via Giulia there is an arch with an inscription praising the emperor Augustus. The amphitheatre of Spello dates from the first century BC.

Spello is a town of winding, sometimes steep streets, little courtyards, and piazze which are often irregular and usually small. Its churches are old and venerable. Santa Maria Maggiore in Piazza Maggiore was built in the late thirteenth century and frescoed at the very beginning of the sixteenth by Pintoricchio. Don't miss the glistening Deruta mosaic floor of the Capella Baglioni. Pintoricchio also contributed to the thirteenth-century church of Sant'Andrea a sinuous painting of the 'Madonna and Child' with various saints. The Piazza della Repùbblica is cooled by a Renaissance fountain and shadowed by the Palazzo Communale. Make your way to the belvedere at the top of the town. Here children play among Roman remains, their grandmothers sitting watching them, close to the Gothic church of Vallegloria and overlooking a tremendous panorama.

From Spello continue north-west, making your way to Assisi by way of San Damiano. Although the crucifix which spoke to St Francis is now in the church of Santa Chiara, Assisi, there is much of beauty and fascination here. The church remains extremely simple, its façade today probably exactly as it was left by St Francis after he had restored it. You can still see the low refectory where St Clare and her nuns used to eat. And the custodians will point to a window from which she reputedly leaned waving a thurible, which so frightened the invading Saracens that they fled.

Prolong your stay at Assisi to make an excursion to two other Umbrian towns, both on the N3, one north of Foligno, one south. Both command spine-tingling panoramic views of this green land, ravishing medieval churches and palaces, as well as rich art galleries. That at Nocera Umbra, which lies to the north, is situated in the late fourteenth-century church of San Francesco and contains superb works by Nicolò Alunno. In that at exquisite Trevi to the south, one of the works by Spagna, illustrating the life of St Francis, charmingly includes in the background a view of his own basilica at Assisi.

Boisterous, beautiful Perugia and a cool oasis

'The situation of the town is beautiful and the view of the lake charming,' wrote Goethe at the end of his visit to Perugia in 1768. Its situation was still beautiful when I first visited Perugia in 1956. This was a chance arrival. I had run almost completely out of money on a trip to Tuscany and Umbria, and hitched a lift with a truck-owner transporting grapes, not really caring where he took me. As we neared the city it seemed a dream-town, rising in the distance in the sunlight.

Today the urban sprawl starts six kilometres outside its walls, and old Perugia on its hill seems like a sinking man, struggling to pull himself out of a filthy swamp. Winding up from the west, you too must struggle through the clinging suburbs to an exquisite city that is rightly twinned with such European gems as Bratislava, Tübingen and Aix-en-Provence. Park in the narrow Borgo XX Giugno and forget the squalid outskirts of Perugia by visiting the monastery and church of San Pietro. Its belfry is as slender as one of the

Virgin Mary's fingers in a picture by Cimabue, rising seventy metres into the sky, designed by Bernardo Rossellino in 1468 and contrasting with the vast cloister entrance which Valentino Martelli designed one and a half centuries later.

Inside the church (the doorway is in the north cloister) you discover you are visiting what amounts to a major art gallery, but only after your eyes have adjusted to the glowing interior. Although San Pietro dates from the late sixteenth to the early seventeenth centuries, a church has stood here since the sixth century. Before that this was the site of a Roman temple, and the lovely rows of arches separating the nave from the two side aisles almost certainly once supported the temple. Above these arches are canvases brought here from Venice in the early seventeenth century, some of them probably by no less a genius than Tintoretto.

The Benedictines of Perugia seem to have forsaken their native Umbrian artists more than once when they reconstructed their monastic church. To create the carved and gilded box-vaulted ceiling they turned in 1564 to a Tuscan sculptor, Benedetto Giovanni Pierantonio from Montepulciano. The two polygonal stone pulpits are lovely pieces of work, carved between 1487 and 1530 by Francesco da Guido, who came from Settignano. Even the exquisite early sixteenth-century choir stalls are only partly Perugian. Bernardino di Luca Antonibi of Perugia worked on them, but he was helped by a woodcarver named Stefano who came from Bologna. And the marble, gilded altar frontal is by Mino da Fiesole. How does one choose between such masterpieces? Of the many frescos and paintings inside San Pietro, the one that delights me most is in the south aisle. It depicts St Peter nonchalantly arresting the fall of a pillar simply by making the sign of the cross.

Leave this cornucopia of artistic treasures and walk up Borgo XX Giugno through the Porta San Pietro, a white marble, monumental semi-ruin which was built in the second half of the fifteenth century to the designs of Agostino di Duccio. You are now in Corso Cavour, to the right of which is one of Perugia's noblest basilicas: the pink and white San Domenico, begun in 1394 and (as you see from its façade) still waiting to be finished.

The Dominicans built their church on the site of Perugia's old horse fair. These holy monks greatly coveted the plenary indulgence that had been granted to the rival Franciscan shrine at Assisi, the Porziuncola, and eventually they achieved one of their own, by persuading the Pope that their church at Perugia housed the corpse of the first Christian martyr, St Stephen – a claim long since abandoned.

Pope Pius II consecrated their basilica in 1458, but the interior as we see it today dates from a re-modelling in the first half of the seventeenth century. By contrast with San Pietro, San Domenico has donated most of its artistic treasures to the national gallery of Perugia, a circumstance which to my mind only serves to make the superb east windows, fired in the fifteenth century, gleam more power-fully since nothing competes with them. San Domenico is very bare inside, save for its extremely ornate organ. For a religious *frisson*, look for a chapel next to the organ decorated with a fourteenth-century picture of two Domini-cans being murdered, beside whom St Sebastian is being vigorously shot at. Look out too for the fourteenth-century Gothic tomb of Pope Benedict XI by Arnolfo di Cambio.

San Domenico is by far the largest church in Perugia, but the Renaissance cloister next to the basilica is gentle and welcoming. It leads to the Umbrian museum of archaeology, whose exhibits spill into the cloister itself. From here Corso Cavour runs upwards to the church of San Ercolano. On either side of the narrow road still narrower streets rise steeply, with houses and shops sometimes on either side. Recently I parked here and was instantly accosted by a Perugian who leapt off his chair on the pavement at my arrival. His job was to prospect for potential guests at a nearby hotel, and when I accepted his invitation he produ-ced a trolley to wheel my baggage up to the hostelry.

San Ercolano seems more a defensive fortress than a

church. This house of God has suffered over the centuries, largely because much of it was demolished to make room for another, greater fortress, the Rocca Paolina; but its early sixteenth-century staircase elegantly contrasts with the dour old fourteenth-century church to whose porch it ascends.

The Rocca Paolina is a symbol of papal temporal power. Its presence also helps to explain why there is no salt in Umbrian bread. After warring with Pope Urban V, the Perugians became subordinate to the papacy with the Treaty of Bologna, signed in 1370. Frequently they disregarded this submission, rebelling against papal delegates and expelling them from the city. Their final act of insubordination occurred in the early sixteenth century when they refused to pay a new salt tax to Pope Paul III. The incensed Pope invaded the city, put down the Perugian rebellion and in 1540 commissioned Aristotile and Antonio Sangallo to build a mighty citadel to keep the Perugians in order. The Rocca was inscribed '*ad coercendam Perusionorum audaciam*'.

Only in the nineteenth century did Perugia free herself from papal rule and become part of the Kingdom of Italy. In 1860 most of the Rocca was demolished, and the offensive inscription done away with. What remains is impressive and includes an Etruscan gateway, the Porta Marzia, which the Sangallo brothers were astute enough to include in their building – an historically judicious decision, for Perugia had been one of the twelve Etruscan confederate cities until it fell into the hands of the Romans in 310 BC.

From here climb a gently sloping set of steps, the Via San Ercolano, and pass through an arch, turning right at the top along Via Guglielmo Oberdan to reach the Piazza Matteotti. If it is morning you will have threaded your way through a street market perched precariously on either side of the street and selling clothing, shoes and jewellery. On the west side of Piazza Matteotti is a covered market, as well as the Palazzo del Capitano del Popolo. Even if you have nothing to buy, visit the market for its panorama of the plain of Assisi.

Built in the 1470s by two architects from Lombardy, the Palazzo del Capitano del Popolo is matched in arrogant splendour by the Tribunali on the right, once the city's university and built between 1472 and 1481. Here the Gothic style gracefully gives way to the Renaissance, as your eye rises from the ogival arches of the ground floor to the windows above. Look out for the architrave embossed with a coat-of-arms supported by two Perugian griffins. It belonged long ago to a hospice dedicated to Our Lady of Mercy.

Now take the Via Fani, which leads out of the Piazza Matteotti and offers at the end a view of the Renaissance doorway of the Gothic Palazzo dei Priori, Perugia's town hall. As you emerge from the narrow street you will spot how delicately the whole end of this palazzo, dating from the late thirteenth century and enlarged in the mid-fifteenth, curves and bows outwards. The whole building becomes more and more graceful as it rises to the skies. Its entrance is guarded by griffins and lions. The former is the mascot of the city; the latter the symbol of the Guelphs. These particular bronzes were booty from the gates of Sienna, taken after the Perugians had defeated the Siennese in 1358.

The Madonna painted over the Renaissance entrance is a delicate masterpiece by Pintoricchio. The first floor includes a magnificent vaulted hall, and the second floor houses Perugia's rich medieval library. Above that is the Galleria Nazionale, the unmissable National Gallery of Umbria, open each day except Monday from 09.00 to 14.00 (closing an hour earlier on public holidays).

Simply to walk through the various rooms of this palace of art is deeply satisfying. The atrium, the hall of the Consiglio Generale, built between 1333 and 1335, sets the whole tone. Room 2 houses the originals of Nicola and Giovanni Pisanos' Romulus and Remus suckled by the she-wolf, which is now replaced by a copy on the great fountain outside. Accompanying them are three delicious marbles by Arnolfo di Cambio, depicting a woman, a man and an old man, all refreshing themselves at a spring.

In room 4 there is a lovely late-Gothic work, Gentile da Fabriano's 'Madonna and Child', a painting which once graced the church of San Domenico. Then (in room 7) you come across one of those inspired hangings that art galleries all too rarely seem to accomplish. Here you can compare the same scene, a 'Madonna and Child with Saints', by two masters: Giotto and Piero della Francesca.

These splendid works of art are really setting the scene for the main reason for visiting the National Gallery of Umbria, namely the works of Perugino and Pintoricchio. Perugino was not a native of this city. His birthplace was Città della Pieve near Chiusi, and his earliest work was done around Florence. He befriended such masters as Verrocchio and Botticelli and soon was noted enough to be travelling from Florence to Rome and Umbria, executing commissions and increasing his fame. In 1475 we know that he painted some frescos for the Palazzo dei Priori, but I would rather not know this, for these frescos are now lost. Two years later he was back in Rome, working on the Sistine Chapel, experimenting with the problems of depicting space in painting. Umbria failed for a time to win him back. Though the priests of Orvieto cathedral even paid him in advance to fresco one of their chapels, in spite of their frequent pleas he never actually did the work.

Slowly, however, Perugia seduced him back. When the Guild of Bankers commissioned Perugino to paint their Collegio del Cambio, he decided to set up his own studio in the city. Soon he was nicknamed the *patriarcha perusino*. His work for the Collegio del Cambio gave him a new lease of artistic and intellectual life, for here he wished to demonstrate that the virtues of antiquity and the inspiration of Jesus are both needed for perfection. Perugino covered part of the ceiling with grotesques imitated from antique models – an innovation copied by many later artists. And he so liked what he had done that he has left us his own self-portrait in the Collegio del Cambio, an image (it seems to me) of a bad-tempered, restless genius whose hot-red hat matches his flushed scarlet cheeks.

Perugino became famous and admired. His two greatest disciples (until the Pre-Raphaelites discovered him in the nineteenth century) were Raphael and Pintoricchio. Pintoricchio was actually born here in Perugia, around the year 1454, but he too spent much time painting in Rome, where he worked alongside Perugino on the frescos of the Sistine Chapel (scholars argue that the 'Baptism of Jesus' there is entirely by him). He learned from Perugino to imitate antiquity and carried the practice even further; and, far more than his master, he loved to apply gilded stucco work to his art.

The influence of Piero della Francesca on the early Perugino is clear enough in his 'Adoration of the Magi' in room 13. By room 14 we are breathing the air of the fully fledged master, with works by his assistants and by Pintoricchio. It is well worth pausing here before Benedetto Bonfigli's banner of St Bernardino of Sienna. Bernardino's preaching technique included holding up a placard with the sign of the name of Jesus, IHS, urging his hearers to turn to this man as their saviour, and Bonfigli has faithfully included this sign in his picture. It is also fascinating in this room to compare the treatment by Perugino and Pintoricchio of two miracles by St Bernardino, the former's painting dazzlingly architectural, the latter's spacious, with the valleys, trees and hills of Umbria in the background.

Next comes room 15, packed with works entirely by the two great Umbrians. They include fragments of a great altarpiece of thirty panels, painted on both sides, which Perugino executed for the church of Sant'Agostino between 1512 and 1523. When the altarpiece was dismantled in 1650 some panels went abroad and others were lost. Giorgio Vasari tells us that Perugino had far more interest in money than in religion, yet his religious art can be deeply moving. The panels preserved here include a magical 'Baptism of Jesus', which happily allows me to quote the lines which T.S. Eliot wrote in 1918:

45

> A painter of the Umbrian school
> Designed upon a gesso ground
> The nimbus of the Baptized God.
> The wilderness is cracked and browned
> But through the water pale and thin
> Still shine the unoffending feet
> And there above the painter set
> The Father and the Paraclete.

Spare time for at least two other rooms in the gallery. Room 23 was formerly the Capella dei Priori, built between 1429 and 1443 and dedicated to St Ercolano. Rightly, therefore, its pictures illustrate the life of the patron saint of Perugia. I especially like the one by Benedetto Bonfigli which depicts a traitor in AD 547 revealing to the besieging Goths the Perugian trick of tossing their last calf stuffed with corn over the wall, to give their enemies the impression that they are well stocked with food, thus persuading them to lift the siege. The Goths are shown cutting up the calf with pikes and spades. St Ercolano, beheaded and buried alongside a little child, is dug up again forty days later and found to be intact. And then his body is translated first to San Pietro, then to the cathedral of San Lorenzo.

Finally, do not miss the 'Madonna and Child' in room 24, a work sculpted for the church of San Francesco al Prato by the Florentine Agostino di Duccio on his visit to Perugia between 1457 and 1461. Mary is wonderfully serene, her large hands caressing and protecting her *bambino*, who stands up, half-smiling, his hair carefully brushed into a little curl that would make any mother proud.

This does not exhaust the riches of Perugia's Palazzo dei Priori. Its colourfully decorated Sala dei Notari is also open to the public (except on Mondays) from 09.00 to 12.00 and from 16.00 to 20.00 (slightly shorter hours in winter) and you enter from Piazza IV Novembre under a bronzed griffin and lion. No one really knows the name of the thirteenth-century master who painted this lovely hall. The question is now fairly academic, for the pictures we see here today derive

from a thoroughgoing restoration carried out by Matteo
Tassi in the 1860s. From mid-October to mid-June the Sala
dei Notari is the venue for entrancing musical evenings.
German, French, American, Italian and British musicians
play and sing music from Bach to Stravinsky, from Scarlatti
to Prokofiev. When the Sala dei Notari is not hosting these
concerts, they take place in the nearby Teatro Communale
Morlacchi, an elegant theatre of 1780, designed by the Perugian architect Alessio Lorenzini. As for the boisterous Perugian jazz festival, it seems to take place everywhere in the
city. Information about these events is available from no. 63
Corso Vannucci (tel. 075 25264/22271).

North of the Palazzo dei Priori stands the mansion and
chapel of the Guild of Bankers (the Collegio del Cambio),
built for them by Bartolomeo di Mattiolo and his assistants in
the mid-fifteenth century and – as we have already noticed –
frescoed by Perugino and members of his studio.

We are now in the Corso Vannucci, named after Pietro
Vannucci, Perugia's most famous artist son, whom everyone
called, and still calls, Perugino. Corso Vannucci is also
celebrated for Sandri's famous coffee shop, owned by the
same family for more than 100 years. Walk left along it into
Piazza Italia, built over the partly demolished Rocca after
Perugia's liberation from the papacy in 1860. The far end of
this walk offers a lovely panorama over the valley and
towards the hills. If you lean over the balcony and peer to the
right, you can just spot a stretch of the ancient Etruscan
wall, which incorporates the Porta Mandorla. To the far left
you can see San Pietro, and almost straight ahead rises the
fretted spire of the convent church of Santa Giuliana. This
fourteenth-century foundation has a distinctly raffish
history, for by the sixteenth century its nuns were leading
lives of phenomenal laxity. The building serenely presided
over it all, with a cloister designed by a brilliant Umbrian
architect whom we shall come across later, Matteo Gattapone.

Stroll back to the Corso Vannucci and the Palazzo dei
Priori, and beyond it to the Piazza IV Novembre, Perugia's

cathedral square. What I remember most vividly from my first visit here is the superb fountain in the centre. In the second half of the thirteenth century the Perugians decided to construct an aqueduct to bring water to their city. This was the well designed to receive the water by Fra Bevignate, who was also architect of the aqueduct. Nicola and Giovanni Pisano were engaged to decorate the fountain with sculptures and to surmount the upper basin with bronze females.

The upper of the two polygonal basins bears two dozen superb allegorical statues. The lower basin is utterly delightful, decorated with scenes from the months of the year, running on into the symbols of contemporary learning (grammar, dialectics, rhetoric, arithmetic, geometry, music, astronomy and philosophy), adding scenes from the Old Testament, and ending with Romulus and Remus and a couple of Aesop's fables. The most delightful of these is the fable of the wolf and the crane. Here is the story in a nineteenth-century English version:

A Wolf had got a bone stuck in his throat, and in the greatest agony ran up and down, beseeching every animal he met to relieve him: at the same time hinting at a very handsome reward to the successful operator. A Crane, moved by his entreaties and promises, ventured her long neck down the Wolf's throat, and drew out the bone. She then modestly asked for the promised reward. To which the Wolf, grinning and showing his teeth, replied with seeming indignation, 'Ungrateful creature! to ask for any other reward than that you have put your head into a Wolf's jaws, and brought it out safe again!'

The moral of the fable is: 'Those who are charitable only in the hope of a return must not be surprised if, in their dealings with evil men, they meet with more jeers than thanks.'

The worldly-wise Pisanos, however, took care to add a more cynical emblem to this basin. A sad lioness watches a man beating her cubs. The motto is: '*Si vis ut timet leo, verbera catulum*' – 'If you want the lion to fear you, bash her little ones', meaning roughly, take on an enemy at his weakest point.

Blessing the fountain is a bronze statue of Pope Julius III, seated in the chair of St Peter beside the cathedral of San Lorenzo. Vincenzo Danti's statue of the pontiff, wearing his triple tiara, his robes swirling around him, sums up perfectly the vigour of this humanist Pope who died after a five-year pontificate which began in 1550. Julius had studied law in Perugia and at Bologna, learned the liberal arts in Rome, studied theology with the Dominicans and become chamberlain of Pope Julius II. Nepotism helped his rise, for in 1511 he had succeeded his uncle as Archbishop of Siponto, but his native talents also assisted him and he was honoured by being asked to preach the sermon when the Fifth Lateran Council reassembled in 1512. Thereafter his rise was swift. He was made a cardinal in 1536 and furthered the Counter-Reformation as co-president of the Council of Trent.

Julius resented the Emperor Charles V's sway in Church matters, and he was instrumental in moving the Council from Trent to Bologna. The emperor took his revenge in 1549 by vetoing Julius's hopes to succeed Paul III as Pope. Julius judiciously compromised and was elected the following year.

Julius carried the family penchant for nepotism into his pontificate, once scandalizing his fellow-Christians by bestowing a cardinal's hat on a 17-year-old relative. Yet he was also a reforming Pope, longing to stop priests and bishops from using the money from benefices without accepting the care of souls that went with these offices. He confirmed the constitution of the newly formed Society of Jesus and founded a Jesuit college. He wished to impose a new strin-gency over monastic discipline, and wanted to reconcile Mesopotamian Nestorians and Abyssinian Copts to the Catholic Church. He longed to send missionaries to the Indies, the Americas and the Far East. In his last year he rejoiced that Mary Tudor had succeeded to the throne of England and that the English Parliament had once again acknowledged papal supremacy.

He died with many of his aspirations unfulfilled. But he had

49

an astute nose for the arts. For my part, whenever I pass his statue by the steps of the cathedral of Perugia, I thank this majestic, if occasionally flawed, churchman for making Giovanni Perluigi da Palestrina choir master of St Peter's, Rome, and for appointing Michelangelo its chief architect.

When you first enter Perugia cathedral you must sit and let your eyes adjust to the dark. Then the painted ceiling emerges from the gloom. A treasure-trove reveals itself: the carved baptistery of 1477; the grille-enclosed chapel of San Bernardino with an overwrought 'Descent from the Cross' and an excellent mid-sixteenth-century stained-glass window; splendid late fifteenth-century choir stalls; a *pietà* and 'God the Father', both by Agostino di Duccio; and, above all, in the Capella del Santo Anello, a golden reliquary containing no less than the wedding ring of the Blessed Virgin Mary, stolen by the Perugians from the city of Chiusi.

The first time I came to Perugia the pillars inside the cathedral were all swathed in velvet, and I was tremendously impressed. I have never seen them so decked since.

Leave the cathedral by the west door, which takes you into the Piazza Dante, and walk round to the south side. Here, in the shade, enterprising traders sell ceramics and terracottas on the steps. Find the arched Via Ulisse Rocchi at the south-east corner of this square and amble down its narrow self. The Pizzeria Etrusca warns that you are approaching Perugia's great Etruscan arch, the Arco d'Agosto, its monumental character slightly belied by the little house with a window and balcony that sits atop it. Even so, the ancient arch is tall, shallow and extremely impressive. From the other side you can easily make out the Etruscan lower structure, built in the third and second centuries BC; the Roman part, inscribed '*Augusta Perusia*' and dating from around AD 45; and the Renaissance loggia above – three ages of Perugian history sitting contentedly one on top of the other.

The pretty pink and white building, an eighteenth-century palazzo, situated immediately beyond the Arco d'Agosto, is now the University for Foreigners. Walk past it up the narrow Corso Garibaldi, anticipating a good ten minutes' uphill walk to reach the astonishingly delicate sixth-century church of Sant'Angelo. Corso Garibaldi is crammed with medieval houses, Renaissance doorways, convents, disused and still active churches, with arched streets running off to right and left. One of these, Via Pinturicchio, is so named because Pintoricchio (whose name can also be spelled Pinturicchio) lived at no. 47.

On the way to Sant'Angelo you pass the church of Sant' Agostino, with a façade satisfyingly composed of brick and pink and white marble. Perugino himself designed its choir stalls, and Baccio d'Angelo faithfully carved and inlaid them in the thirty years from 1502. Adjoining this church is an oratory whose seventeenth-century gilded ceiling is riotously extravagant.

Next appears the monastery of the Blessed Columba, where (according to the wall plaque) St Francis of Assisi met St Domenico di Guzman. They did not meet in the present building, which dates from the mid-sixteenth century and was designed by Galeazzo Alessi to house the pious bones of a Perugian mystic who died in 1501. To add to the artistic wealth of this unprepossessing street, on the opposite corner from this monastery, as you turn right, you find a little passage leading to the monastery Clarisse Santa Agnese – dedicated to St Clare's sister – where, between 09.00 and 11.00 and 15.00 and 18.00, you can admire a fresco by Perugino.

Pass under an archway and turn right to walk up Via del Tempio as far as the grassy surroundings of Sant'Angelo. Constructed on the site of a pagan temple, and cannibalizing some of its materials, Sant'Angelo is an exquisite, tiny round building. Inside, brick vaults spring from the walls to meet in the centre of the dome, and a circle of white marble pillars holds everything up. As an inscription on the altar indicates, even this holy table came from the pagan temple.

Now is the time to picnic, sitting on the ancient excavated

51

stones on the lawn or under one of the shady trees, before making your way down the steps which lead by a vineyard to the battlemented Porta Sant'Angelo. What I like about this fourteenth-century gateway is the way you can make out various stages in its building, because the Perugians did not mind successively changing the material they used: sandstone at the bottom, white stone half-way up and brick to finish the job.

From here Via Zefferino Faina winds down to Piazza Università, named after the University of Perugia which is housed in this square in a monastery that once belonged to the Olivetani order. Walk past the university to reach Via Santa Elisabetta, turning right along it. Our route runs now by way of Via Pascoli past the fourteenth-century church of San Matteo (with its most appealing belfry) as far as the once mighty church of San Francesco. A landslide brought the thirteenth-century San Francesco to its knees, but its façade remains intact. Next to it stands a delightful building, the renowned oratory of San Bernardino. The façade is richly coloured, its bas-reliefs sculpted by Agostino di Duccio. St Bernardino of Sienna had come here as a missionary in the first half of the fifteenth century and made such a powerful impression that the Perugians decided to build this oratory in his honour the moment he was canonized in 1450. If you go inside, note that its main altar happens to be a third-century sarcophagus.

Now make your way south from the piazza to arrive at the Porta Trasima, originally an Etruscan gateway though Gothicized in the fourteenth century. Beside it rises yet another entrancing church, the Renaissance Madonna del Luce. The thirteenth-century façade incorporates a double doorway and another characteristic Umbrian rose window. Inside is a fine marble tabernacle sculpted by a monk, Frater Ferrucci, in 1487.

From here Via dei Priori will take you back up into the centre of the city and the Palazzo dei Priori. Let me insist now that in no way do I claim that this tour has revealed every treasure of the city, not even every great palazzo, amazing panorama or superb church. There is much more to explore in Perugia, many medieval nooks and crannies, with trattorie and restaurants hidden around corners and down alleyways, with stones used and re-used since Etruscan times, crumbling but still faithfully serving the citizens. But it is time to wander outside its walls.

The road from Perugia to Torgiano winds fifteen kilometres south-east. The antiquity of Torgiano is indicated by its very name, meaning Tower of Janus, the Roman god who faced both ways. I once stayed here at a superb hotel called Le Tre Vasselle, a sixteenth-century inn which has been entirely modernized inside without losing any of its character outside. Le Tre Vasselle runs several cookery classes annually, using the herbs from its own garden and the rich produce of the surrounding countryside, and when I had the pleasure of eating in its restaurant with Signora Simona Fanelli of Promotour Umbria she insisted, 'If you come to Umbria you must become fat. It's compulsory.'

There are today five areas of Umbria producing wine officially classed as DOC (*denominazione di origine controllata*), that is, officially protected and controlled with regard to their origin. These are the wines of Montefalco, those from the region of Città di Castello, the wines of Orvieto, the wines grown by Lake Trasimeno and finally the wines of Torgiano. You can taste and buy them (and lesser wines) in any Umbrian *enoteca*, or vintage wine merchant. But to my mind the greatest wine treat is to visit the Cantina Lungarotti which produces the wines of Torgiano.

The law of 1968 regulating the DOC wines of Torgiano laid down that the reds must be ruby in colour, delicate and vinous in aroma, brilliant in clarity, and from the point of view of taste dry, harmonious and of good body. As for the whites, their colour should be a strawy yellow, the aroma light and pleasing as well as vinous, their clarity again brilliant, and their taste light, fruity but appealingly sharp. If these requirements seem a demanding mouthful, the qualities of the wines of the Cantina Lungarotti are yet more subtle and the demands of the vintners yet more exacting.

There are altogether a dozen table wines produced by this house. The wine called Torre di Giano is made solely from the Trebbiano and Grechetto grapes, and its colour gleams like golden straw. In Torgiano itself this wine is often served as an aperitif, chilled and invigorating. A second white, Chardonnay di Miralduolo, derives its name from the grape used (Chardonnay) and the region where these are grown (the Miralduolo vineyards). Again I have always drunk it chilled, but this time usually with a main course, sniffing its bouquet to make my taste buds leak wildly. White Pinot Grigio from the Cantina Lungarotti again indicates by its name that here we have a drink created from one variety of grape (*Pinot gris*), a successful import into Umbria from more northern lands. The house recommends its Pinot Grigio with fish or as an aperitif, and a very aromatic aperitif it makes.

Buffalone is the fourth white Cantina Lungarotti wine, less yellow than Torre di Giano, with a wicked kick that amply justifies its label, which depicts a riot of tipsy Bacchanals. If the alcohol content of these white wines is proving too heady, you can always move on to Lungarotti's sparkling Rondo. Other whites include a Chardonnay 'Vigna i Palazzi', and a white Torre di Giano produced from grapes from one sole vineyard and designed to be drunk after maturing for four or five years or so.

The cellar's most famous red wine is called Rubesco, and was one of the first to be given the *appellation* DOC in 1968. Here the grapes, all grown in this region, are of the Sangiovese and Canajolo varieties. It is pleasing to note that the labels incorporate the scene of a grape harvest carved on Perugia's great fountain. As with his special Torre di Giano, Signor Lungarotti also produces a yet more refined version of the Rubesco, created from grapes grown entirely in one vineyard. At Cantina Lungarotti you can also sample a fine rosé wine, Rosata di Brufa, made out of Sangiovese and Canajolo grapes grown around the ancient Castelo Grifone.

The naming of wines is itself a fine art. San Giorgio is one of the finest red wines of the house, and its label reproduces a painting by Raphael showing St George slaying the dragon. A bottle of Lungarotti San Giorgio, far from slaying the judicious drinker, perks up the most depressed spirit. If, on the other hand, I wished simply to toddle off to bed, merry yet still stable, I should better drink among Cantina Lungarotti's reds either the gentle Rosciano or the more robust Cabernet Sauvignon di Miralduolo.

Torgiano boasts not only this celebrated vintner but also its own wine museum – thirteen exhibition rooms in the splendid medieval Palazzo Baglioni. Archaeology and history, the techniques of wine-making, the skills of the cooper and glass-blower, the lore of wine in art, the innkeeper's profession, are all celebrated in this palace; and in case one might balk at such dedication to alcoholic drink (which in excess can, after all, harm us human beings), here there is also a section devoted to the medicinal value of wine.

Down the street from the hotel Le Tre Vasselle you turn right to find a shop selling ceramics, decorated in the traditional patterns of Umbria. Next door is the workshop where they are made. I went inside and found two men working. One told me that he used only clay from the local mountains, throwing it on his potter's wheel before firing it at many thousands of degrees in the kiln. His friend smiled, and carried on polishing and painting fired pots, while over the radio came the voice of Frank Sinatra singing 'Georgia on my mind'.

The streets of Torgiano are flanked by ancient stone and brick houses, many of them guarded by ancient, toothless ladies sitting on chairs by the doorways. The hill town boasts an imposing classical brick and stone church, dedicated to San Bartolomeo and inscribed over the porch with the date MDCCXCVIID. The interior, also eighteenth-century, lives up to the splendid exterior. The font must have come from an older building on this site. In one corner stands a dusty processional *baldacchino*, graced by two cherubs so chubby that one wonders when they last took some exercise.

Corso Vittorio Emanuele leads round the left-hand side of the church where rises its powerful, yet graceful campanile, the bells visible as you look up. If you walk on into the shady Piazza Giacomo Matteotti you see that the belfry rises straight up from the town walls. Over the valley, across rows and rows of vines, you can make out Bettona.

Before we drive there, take the E7 south from Torgiano to Deruta, the majolica capital of Umbria (and seat of the state Institute of Ceramics). Situated by the River Tiber – by whose waters you can take a refreshing beer or glass of wine – Deruta has not confined itself to the patterns of antiquity in producing its ceramics, though if you want a superb amphora this is the place to buy one. Its twentieth-century artists also produce richly decorated plates and vases that clamour to be laden with salads and fruits and, to my mind, would also grace the wall of any kitchen.

Deruta has existed since Roman times. The first historical record of its ceramics occurs in a document of 1387. In this peaceful little town it is difficult to imagine today that in 1500 Cesare Borgia could have attacked it and that in 1534 Braccio Baglione managed to sack it.

To see the majolicas of the past, make your way to the Piazza dei Consoli and Deruta's medieval town hall (or Palazzo Communale). Its three mullioned windows are Romanesque, and on its first floor, alongside local paintings, Etruscan vases and frescos, you can admire the superb workmanship of long-dead local potters. Apart from these the gallery's prize is a 'Madonna and Saints' painted in 1457 by Nicolò Alunno.

Facing the town hall is the fourteenth-century church of San Francesco, with a slender campanile, a pretty cloister whose arches cannot make up their mind whether to be monumental or human in scale, a rose window and, inside, fourteenth-century frescos as well as more Deruta majolicas. The finest fresco is undoubtedly Fiorenzo di Lorenzo's late fifteenth-century picture of God the Father, who is depicted flanked by St Roch and St Sebastian.

Drive three and a half kilometres north along the E7 and turn right for Bettona. Its main square is blessed with a fine church inscribed with the date MDCCIIIIC and dedicated to San Crispolto, but this is not Bettona's finest, in spite of boasting a classical clock set in a classical tower and a campanile so ancient that it requires iron supports to hold it together. Walk on to see the unfussed Romanesque façade of the thirteenth-century church of Santa Maria Maggiore (which I have never managed to get into).

The whole ensemble of Bettona breathes the Middle Ages, with its archways and corridors, its ancient stone and brick houses, its steps and alleyways, its pantile roofs. Via degli Archi to the north of the eighteenth-century church beckons suggestively, as the Italians put it. Resist and go the other way from the church, and you pass cloisters and a deep well. You walk through another arch into a tree-shaded piazza where you can sit and drink a glass of wine looking out over the medieval walls towards a vast olive-bedecked panorama.

Bettona is a town of a thousand cats, most of them asleep by the roadside. The civic art gallery, housed in the medieval Palazzo del Podestà and reached up an external flight of steps, contains works by Perugino and Tiberio d'Assisi as well as terracottas by Della Robbia. The palazzo itself is adorned with sculpted coats of arms and rises above a welcome bar, pleasingly set in the former cellars.

Take the winding road from Bettona north-east to Passagio. Here stands a former monastery which has been adapted as a factory. Some say the crypt of its church predates the eleventh century. Drive on to Bastia, which lies on the left bank of the River Chiascio. This industrial town played a crucial role in the dangerous years when St Clare of Assisi was desperately seeking to escape the demands of her father, for here (in what is now the cemetery church of San Paolo) she took refuge in the monastery of San Paolo delle Abbadesse after her consecration at the Porziuncola. The thirteenth-century church of Santa Croce in Piazza Mazzini is also well worth a visit, especially for the many artistic treasures it shelters.

The swift route 75 leads back to Perugia, but for a refreshing contrast with the built-up city you can bypass Perugia and follow route 75(bis) north-west and then turn north and visit the exquisite hill town of Corciano. Corciano is said to have been founded by a companion of Ulysses who had sailed up the Tiber. From where you park, outside the medieval walls, you can gaze across the motorway for a vista of rolling hills, which include Mount Sperello and Mount Merlino, their ridges becoming bluer in the distance. The white walls of Corciano gleam in the sun, warmed by the interspersed pink and ochre bricks and sometimes, too, by pink and ochre stones.

As so often in these Umbrian hill towns, as you walk around the ramparts you discover arched passageways leading up through the walls to the centre. Climb the steps from Corciano's parking place and walk right around the walls to reach a fortified medieval gateway. Then climb up the steps through the Arco della Vittoria. The whole town is immaculate (even a trifle antiseptic). Half-way up, the steps curve and on your right rises a medieval tower topped by a campanile added in 1864. It belongs to the church of Santa Maria Assunta, a classical building erected in 1870.

In Corciano pretty ceramic plaques identify and often date the most charming and historic of the buildings, such as the fifteenth-century house of the Capitano del Contado, who represented the town at Perugia. Here there are occasional references to the celebrated inhabitants of yesteryear. One such plaque notes the birthplace of Cardinal Luigi Rotelli (1833–1901). Another indicates the well where he played as a boy. He became Bishop of Montefiascino, Papal Nuncio in Paris and now has a street in Corciano named after him.

Above me rose another ancient tower, and an old man who seemed yet more ancient plodded down the street, helped by a gnarled walking-stick, his eyes glistening with moisture. For more than a quarter of a century this town has been kept in spanking condition, for beginning on the first Sunday of August it hosts a fourteen-day festival of classical music, with torchlight processions and much eating and drinking. In the Piazza dei Caduti, overlooked by a walled garden sporting lemon trees, I took a glass of wine and met an Italian who, he said, had been born in London – the son of the old man of the watery eyes, who was now slumped over his own wine in a corner of the café. His father, he said, was 106 years old. 'I like living here nowadays,' this Italian-Cockney told me, adding, 'Of course, if I were still eighteen years old, I'd like living in London better.'

Leave Corciano by the north-west, driving to Mantignana and turning here for lovely Castel Rigone. The route winds up through olive groves, woods and vineyards, with entrancing views of valleys and hills. Umbria's valleys are often dotted with farmhouses (a good number of them abandoned) which do not huddle together as villages but simply remain within shouting distance of each other – evidence that this region of Italy has experienced not only turmoil but also periods of peace when people had no need to cling together for self-defence. In other places, villages cluster on top of a hill around a fortress, as at Castel Rigone, where the thirteenth-century Rocca is today an appealing ruin. The church of the Madonna del Miracoli here is one of Umbria's least-known and most effective Renaissance buildings, begun in 1494, boasting a doorway sculpted in 1512 and frescoed by pupils of Perugino. Castel Rigone is a fine place to buy terracotta pottery.

I love driving from here north-east across the ridges and past vineyards as far as Umbértide. Mount Acuto, 926 metres above sea-level, suddenly appears as a rounded hump with scarcely any vegetation, especially on its north side, the rocks prised out and quarried. Next to it rises Mount Murlo, some 818 metres above sea-level. Villages such as Rigonella appear, a few houses wrapped around a church. But to take that route would lead us far out of our planned way, which is to encircle the region of Umbria around Perugia. Instead, take the road which runs due south from Castel Rigone to the walled town of Magione. As you descend the route offers splendid views of Lake Trasimeno.

Magione overlooks both the lake and a plain known as the Pian da Carpine. The word Carpine refers to the many hornbeams growing here. Magione means simply 'dwelling place', but the name has a more romantic origin. Situated at a crossroads of roads leading from Perugia, Cortona, Chiusi and Arezzo, the township was developed in the Middle Ages by the Knights Hospitallers of St John of Jerusalem. Here they set up a hospice for pilgrims which they called the Magione del Pian da Carpine. In the thirteenth century the Perugians, spotting the township's strategic importance, built here the Lambardi tower to assert their authority over the district.

Today Magione is endowed not only with a fourteenth-century castle, which Fieravante Fieravanti of Bologna built for the Knights Hospitallers on the site of their hospice, but also with a fine park, children's swings, seats, slides and a well-preserved World War II fighter plane. The castle incorporates a Romanesque abbey. The parish church of Magione was rebuilt in the nineteenth century by Luigi Poletti and frescoed by Gerardo Dottori in 1947. The church of the Madonna delle Grazie dates from 1209 and was restored in 1955. I find it instructive to compare Dottori's modern frescos in the nineteenth-century church with the delicate 'Madonna and Angels' painted by Angelo da Orvieto for the old church in 1371.

After this wealth of history you are not surprised to learn that towards the end of the twelfth century Brother Giovanni del Pian da Carpine was born at Magione and became the first Westerner ever to describe Mongolia and give an account of its history. Pope Innocent IV had sent him east as envoy to the Tartars and the Great Khan, and his account precedes the more famous one by Marco Polo.

Turn right here along route 75(bis) to make a leisurely trip around Umbria's greatest lake (in fact the largest in central

Italy). Lago Trasimeno has a surface of 182 square kilometres. The Etruscans were the first to develop the lake, when they began reclaiming the Pian da Carpine. An underground stream built by the Romans and another canal constructed in the nineteenth century supplement the rivulets that once were all that filled the lake. One of these little streams is called Sanguinetto, in memory of the time it flowed with Roman blood, for in the marshlands around this lake Hannibal in 217 BC vanquished a Roman army led by the consul Flaminius.

Hannibal had marched across the Arno, devastating the countryside. Reaching Lake Trasimeno, he invested the heights above Passignano sul Trasemino and Borghetto. Flaminius disastrously supposed his enemy to be marching on Rome. The day of battle dawned foggy and damp, and Flaminius rashly exposed his left flank and his rearguard to Hannibal's troops. By the time the battle was over, Flaminius was dead and Hannibal had slaughtered 15,000 of his soldiers. Some of the Romans were decapitated as they sank helplessly in the mud.

This was by no means the last time that Lake Trasimeno and its region were fought over, for Perugians, Florentines, the papacy and the Grand Dukes of Tuscany vied with each other for control of it. The Perugians achieved their aim in the Middle Ages, but with their decline the papacy took over. Finally in 1860 the whole region voted to join the Kingdom of Italy.

The architectural legacy of these battles is seen in the countless keeps and castles which festoon the region – at Agello, Montesperello, Sant'Arcangelo, Monte Colognola, Borghetto, Montemelino – all of them still keeping a wary eye for long-dead enemies. The people of Chiusi erected a tower on the road to Perugia which they called Becchetequillo ('What about this?'), at which the Perugians built one facing it called Becchetequello ('What about that?'), and the two towers still glare angrily at one another.

Passignano sul Trasimeno is today both a holiday resort

with a lovely beach and an ancient medieval village at its heart. The village is surrounded by battlemented walls. From here the Umbrians like to be ferried by boat to two of the islands in the middle of the lake. Nobody lives on the smallest island, Isola Minore. The largest island is Polvese and is linked by ferry to Passignano, Tuoro, Castiglione del Lago and San Feliciano, as well as to Isola Maggiore.

The warm sandstone of Polvese's ruined Romanesque church of San Secondo, which belonged to the Olivetan monks until Pope Gregory XVI abolished the order in 1833, glows in the sun. At the opposite corner of the island is a forsaken castle built in the fourteenth century to defend Polvese against the armies of Arezzo and Sienna. Nearly 10,000 olive trees are farmed here for their oil, and today the wildfowl are protected in the Polvese bird sanctuary. The Perugians, who own this island, have created a long sandy beach. And since the lake is rich in perch, pike, dace, carp and eel (and in fact supplies 30 per cent of Italy's fish), fishermen ply their ancient trade alongside amateur anglers.

Polvese boasts a restaurant which, like all those surrounding Lake Trasimeno, specializes in fish. Local traditions roast fish over open fires, giving particular flavours by using different types of wood and even reeds or gorse in the process. Oddly enough, more typical than these fish dishes are the pork, poultry and game dishes served in this region. The restaurants around Lake Trasimeno are also the only ones I have ever encountered which make turnip tops palatable, enriching them with cream or olive oil.

The island most redolent of Umbria's past is Isola Maggiore, for here in 1211 St Francis landed with only two loaves of bread to eat. He stayed for forty days and consumed no more than half of one of them. The church of San Salvatore on the island dates from the thirteenth century and inside is an 'Annunciation' of 1575 and a fifteenth-century Siennese painting. Further inland you come across the fourteenth-century Gothic church of San Michele Arcangelo, with its numerous frescos and an altar crucifix painted on wood by

Bartolomeo Caporali around 1460.

Drive on through Tuoro and Borghetto and turn south to reach Castiglione del Lago. The town rises from the low-lying land on a promontory jutting out over the lake, the long grey crenellated and turreted curtain-wall of its castle guarding one end of the town, the church the other end. Below Castiglione del Lago a tiny element of holiday grottiness has developed, though not too much. Here there are rooms to let, apartments, hotels, with sandy beaches and grassy banks, boating, fishermen sitting on the rocks and all kinds of recreational facilities – camping, tennis, basketball, archery, trampolining ... The main town, with its castle, its Palazzo Communale and its Palazzo Ducale (respectively by Giovanni Alessi and Jacopo Barozzi da Vignola) snootily seems to keep itself apart from all this activity. Beyond it rises a fine panorama of distant blue ranges of hills, some of them no more threatening than the humps of a camel, others rather grand. One way of enjoying these hills, away from the usually crowded summer beaches of Lake Trasimeno, is to take the road from Tuoro over the mountains to Umbértide, a route which also affords entrancing views of the lake, with pines and little woods leading down to the water by way of orchards, olive groves and vineyards.

I must suggest you resist this temptation to wander off over the mountains to Umbértide. Instead drive south-east from Castiglione del Lago to reach the ancient hill town of Panicale. Guarded by medieval walls, sleepy Panicale lives off handicrafts, such as lace- and furniture-making. Its centre is still protected by massive walls and a couple of powerful gateways. Piazzo Umberto I is exquisite of an evening as the lights come on, and you sit outside the Bar Gallo sipping wine and gazing across the piazza and its fountain at the apse of the magnificent collegiate church. Here too is the town hall, covered with carved stone coats of arms. Then walk to the thirteenth-century Palazzo del Podestà, built out of rough, chocolate-coloured stone and lightened by a couple of delicate mullioned windows. Seek out too the nineteenth-century theatre designed by Giovanni Caproni of Perugia, and especially (outside the walls) the church of San Sebastiano, for inside are two superb frescos by Perugino himself.

Now drive west for another gem, the medieval village of Paciano. If the views from Panicale are impressive, that from Paciano of the three lakes of Trasimeno, Chiusi and Montepulciano is astounding. Paciano is still walled; its church of San Carlo boasts a fine sixteenth-century doorway; and a ruined Franciscan convent and the Torre di Orlando speak of its former religious and strategic importance.

A road runs west from Paciano to join the main route 71, on its way to the Tuscan/Umbrian border. Just before the border the route turns south-east towards Città della Pieve, the red-brick, walled city where Perugino was born, which stands on a ridge overlooking the Tuscan hills. The Etruscans spotted the strategic value of this site, as did Charlemagne, who gave it to the Pope. The mighty Rocca, three of whose towers still stand, rises in Piazza Matteotti. Here in 1503 Count Paolo Orsini and the Duke of Gravina were strangled on the orders of Cesare Borgia after they had taken part in one of the many conspiracies against him.

In 1601 Pope Clement VII declared the town a city and its name was changed from Castel della Pieve to Città della Pieve. Its cathedral, dedicated to Saints Gervasio and Protasio, had been founded in the twelfth century but was transformed as Città della Pieve prospered in the sixteenth and seventeenth. Its walls are marbled, its interior filled with superb works of art, including in the first chapel to the left of the entrance a 'Baptism of Jesus' painted in 1510 by Perugino. Four years later he painted another masterpiece for this cathedral, depicting the Madonna and child with four saints (Peter, Paul and the two to whom the cathedral is dedicated). Another moving piece of religious art hangs in the opposite chapel to the one housing Perugino's 'Baptism', a crucifixion sculpted in the first half of the seventeenth century by Giambologna's pupil Pietro Tacca.

The cathedral at Città della Pieve boasts two towers, an

ancient Romanesque one on the west side, slightly at odds with the lie of the main building, and a classical one built in 1781 at the south-east corner. Crumbling walls and fine palaces abound in the city, among them Alessi's Palazzo Bandini in Piazza del Plebiscito and, at the corner of Via Pietro Vannucci, the sixteenth-century Palazzo della Corgna. From here take Via della Corgna on the right to reach the oratory of Santa Maria dei Bianchi, frescoed with Perugino's magical 'Adoration of the Magi'. Another work by Città della Pieve's greatest son, this time a 'Deposition of Christ', is found in the Gothic church of Santa Maria dei Servi, just outside the walls.

Perugia is forty-three kilometres from Città della Pieve, by way of the route 220 just south-east of the city. The road passes through woodlands and olive groves, and after nine kilometres Piegaro rises on the right. Its parish church, San Silvestro, treasures a crucifix which oozed blood in 1738. The route now runs alongside the River Nestore as far as Tavernelle. Not two kilometres north of here is a secluded sanctuary, dedicated to the Madonna di Mongiovino and built in the early sixteenth century, while just over two kilometres south-east of Tavernelle is yet another such sanctuary, this one dedicated to the Madonna delle Grondici and a century older than the first.

Soon on the left rises first Colle San Paolo, whose modern parish church conceals a tenth-century Romanesque crypt, and then the little hill village of Fontignano, with its turreted castle and a church of the Annunciation sheltering a 'Madonna and Child' painted by Perugino the year before he died. The same church once possessed his very last work, another 'Adoration of the Magi', but somehow this found its way to the National Gallery in London.

Of all the little settlements on the way from Città della Pieve to Perugia the one I most recommend is Agello. Look out for the road on the left which winds charmingly up to it through cypresses. The steps of the Via del Castello curve up to the ruined white blocks of its former church. A hat of bricks holds the bells of its white stone clock-tower. Where the chancel and apse once stood there are now children's swings and seats under the trees. Begonias abound. You can peer down the well in front of the church, before walking up to the restored castle, where the views from the walls are stupendous. One October afternoon at five o'clock the place seemed deserted. Suddenly the large church bell struck five and a little bell beside it began to ring wildly. Who was pulling the rope?

An old man joined me, and I said that Agello seemed like a ghost town. 'There's life in the lower town,' he replied, 'but I call it tranquil here.' It seemed a pity to leave that tranquillity for the elegant but crowded streets of Perugia.

From Orvieto to the hill town of Todi

Winding between banks of wild flowers, past pine trees, spruce and acacia, with poppies in May and June dotting the fields and of course roses and vineyards galore, the road from Viterbo to Orvieto lulls you into happiness without giving warning that the sudden sight of Orvieto itself is one of the most spectacular in all Europe.

The first view of the town across the valley of the River Paglia is breathtaking, so that you almost fail to take the sharp right turn that starts you curving right and left down to the city walls. The cathedral proudly tops the rest of the city, the whole magically balanced on a great outcrop of volcanic rock. Towers and churches, houses and palaces, pinnacles and the rock itself blend into a harmonious pink so subtle that you can hardly bear waiting to negotiate another bend in the road for a further look. You can make out the belfry and church of San Francesco, the Torre del Moro, the Palazzo del Capitano del Popolo and the Papal Palace. Then the road starts to climb again, twisting steeply by the massive city walls which blend into the soft volcanic rock of the tufa itself.

People have lived here since the Bronze Age, and then Orvieto became an important Etruscan centre. Outside the city, at each corner of the roughly triangular rock, are Etruscan remains – a temple to the north-west, the Cannicella tomb to the north-east, and the Tomba del Crocifisso del Tufo to the south – and many of the city's churches are built over the sites of Etruscan temples. Then, in 263 BC, the Romans destroyed Orvieto. Slowly men and women reoccupied the magnificent site, and by the sixth century the Goths dominated the town. In AD 537 Belisarius conquered it for Byzantium.

Life gradually improved. The Lombards overcame the town towards the end of the same century. Soon Orvieto had a bishop and was the stronghold of counts. When Otto III, Holy Roman Emperor, promoted a religious revival in Italy, the counts of Orvieto were ready to found monasteries and churches in the surrounding countryside. By the eleventh century Orvieto had set itself up as a commune. The papacy tried to resist this move towards independence, but eventually Pope Hadrian IV was obliged to acknowledge the city's autonomy.

At the same time Orvieto strongly supported the Guelphs, the papal party, in the struggle against the Ghibellines, who supported the Hohenstaufens of Swabia. In 1199 the Pope nominated as chief magistrate the city's first *podestà*, or leader, Pietro Paranzo. The Ghibelline followers of the emperors Friedrich I and Heinrich IV repeatedly attacked Orvieto and were repeatedly repulsed, although inside the city itself the powerful Filippeschi family espoused the Ghibelline cause and their supporters killed Pietro Paranzo.

These strife-ridden years saw the foundation of Orvieto's medieval heart, as the noblemen built palaces and homes for themselves and their servants, as well as churches to ensure their own salvation. Continually the papacy tried to reestablish itself here. Pope Martin IV filled the city with his fellow-Frenchmen and women from 1281 to 1284, to the intense annoyance of the Italians. The Filippeschi were driven out of the city in 1313. In 1334 Ermanno, a son of the leading Guelph family in Orvieto (the Monaldeschi), took power and brought peace to the city; and twenty years later Cardinal Egidio Albornoz invested the town, annexing it to the papal states. In times of later strife the whole papal court would subsequently move out of Rome and seek refuge here.

For his master, Pope Innocent VI, Albornoz built a fortress at Orvieto, part of which still stands at the eastern corner of the city, though today it has been laid out as a public park. Just beyond it is another pretty park which turns out to incorporate the excavated ruins of an Etruscan temple, known today as the Belvedere. Between the two you find an avenue of trees which takes you down to one of Orvieto's most curious survivals: an artesian well dug on the orders of Pope Clement VII when he took refuge here after the sack of Rome in 1527. He commissioned a fellow-Florentine, Antonio Sangallo the Younger, to build it.

This well (the Pozzo di San Patrizio), dedicated to St Patrick, is thirty-two metres deep and nearly fourteen metres wide. A couple of concentric spiral staircases, each with 248 steps, lead up and down, never meeting or crossing. Each is lit by seventy windows, and the steps were made deliberately shallow so that beasts of burden could trudge down them for a drink. Though presented as one of Orvieto's main tourist attractions, I still find it slightly unnerving to trundle down this deep hole and back up again, especially as the temperature falls alarmingly the deeper you descend.

In Etruscan times Orvieto had but one entrance, cut through the volcanic tufa on the west side of the city and corresponding with today's Porta Maggiore. Its latest acquisition is the statue of Pope Boniface VIII, placed in its niche in 1924. The city gate leads into Via della Cava (or 'quarry'), a reference to this ancient slicing through the rock, and this in turn takes you as far as Via Filippeschi, which leads past the Palazzo Mancini on the left into Orvieto's Piazza della Repubblica. The piazza is charming, yet I never stop here on arriving at Orvieto but hurry on to reach the cathedral. Straight across the piazza is the swiftest route, by way of the fashion, leather, jewellery and cuddly toy shops of the Corso Cavour, ignoring its bars and turning right at the Torre del Moro. You pass the Palazzo Gualterio, which Simone Mosca designed in the early sixteenth century. It sports a massive Renaissance doorway designed by Ippolito Scalza in the seventeenth century.

It is perhaps foolish to rush up such a lovely street – few places in the world contain a main post office built inside a thirteenth-century palace. The medieval Torre del Moro used to be called the papal tower, but changed its name when jousters attached a saracen's head to it for target practice. In 1316 the twenty-four guilds of Orvieto paid for a new bell, which still chimes the hours and bears their coats of arms. And just round the corner in Via della Greca you can read a lapidary inscription bearing Dante's invective against the rival families both of Verona and Orvieto:

> *Vieni a veder Montecchi e Cappelletti,*
> *Monaldi e Filippeschi, uom senze cura;*
> *colo già tristi, e questi con sospetti.*

> (Come, see the Capulets and Montagues,
> The Filippeschi and Monaldeschi, men caring for nought;
> Those plunged in grief, these racked with suspicion.)

From the Torre del Moro, the Via Duomo leads to the cathedral square. There it emerges, its façade one of the acknowledged masterpieces of Italian Gothic, the Romanesque side walls and apse austerely striped in muted green and white as if they were deliberately reigning themselves in so as not to clash with the superabundantly ornate pinks, blues, greens and gold of the façade. Its golden-based mosaics gleam, its crockets bristle, its pilasters twist and in the centre is a chunky rose window.

The curious origin of Orvieto cathedral is often forgotten. This masterpiece would not exist but for the most abstruse medieval theological speculation and a scarcely credible miracle. In the mid-thirteenth century the most acute theologians of the time wrestled with the problem of transubstantiation: how was the substance of bread and wine at the Christian Eucharist converted into the substance of the body and blood of Jesus? That it was so converted no Western Christians had been allowed to doubt since 1215, when the Lateran Council declared the doctrine *de fide*; but no one had satisfactorily managed to elaborate the precise philosophical basis of this conversion until St Thomas Aquinas's *Summa Theologica* gained virtual universal acceptance.

St Thomas's patron, Pope Urban IV, was in Orvieto in 1263, a year before the first part of the *Summa Theologica* appeared, and so was St Thomas himself. In that very year the Pope instructed St Thomas to write a liturgy for the newly instituted Feast of Corpus Christi. In response Aquinas composed that remarkable hymn, 'Pange lingua, gloriosi Corporis mysterium':

> Of the glorious body telling,
>   O my tongue, its mysteries sing,
> And the blood, all price excelling,
>   Which the world's eternal King,
> In a noble womb once dwelling,
>   Shed for this world's ransoming.

The second half of this hymn proceeds to assert the real presence of Christ in the bread and wine of the Eucharist:

> Therefore we, before him bending,
>   This great Sacrament revere;
> Types and shadows have their ending,
>   For the newer rite is here;
> Faith, our outward sense befriending,
>   Makes the inward vision clear.

To this intensely creative moment of theological speculation we owe Orvieto cathedral. The excitement so affected Christians that sacred hosts were miraculously discovered throughout Europe. Those who could not believe in the recently elaborated doctrine of transubstantiation agonized

71

for years. In the selfsame year that Urban IV commissioned St Thomas Aquinas to write his Eucharistic office just such a doubter, a Bohemian priest named Peter, had travelled from Prague to St Peter's, Rome, to beg on the tomb of St Peter himself for the gift of faith. He returned by way of Bolsena, just outside Orvieto. There, as he said Mass in the crypt of the church of Santa Cristina, his prayers were answered. As he raised the sacred Host which he had just consecrated, enough blood poured from it to stain the corporal, that square piece of linen placed under the chalice over the ordinary altar cloth. Transubstantiation was seemingly proven. The blood of Jesus had poured from a piece of bread.

Urban IV ordered that this corporal, now a relic of enormous value, should be brought to Orvieto. To house it, the citizens decided to build their stupendous cathedral. They demolished two other churches in the city centre, and on 13 November 1290 Urban IV's successor, Pope Nicholas IV, laid the first stone where they had stood.

Although the design was probably by Arnolfo di Cambio, the first builder of Orvieto cathedral was Fra Bevignate of Perugia. By a paradoxical stroke of good fortune, the Orvietans employed a local builder named Giovanni Uguccione who proved incompetent. Before the cathedral was finished, it started falling down. The alarmed citizens called in a Siennese architect and sculptor named Lorenzo Maitani, and to him we owe the famous façade and most of its exquisite reliefs.

The excitement of the thirteenth-century theological debate has faded; the thrill of the cathedral built to celebrate it remains. Maitani designed a façade whose basic structure corresponds to that of many churches we have already seen in Umbria. Four polygonal towers divide it into three sections which mirror the nave and aisles inside.

At the bottom of these four pillars are carved the most delicate bas-reliefs. They repay the most minute scrutiny. The first pillar, on the left, illustrates the ancient stories of the Creation and the fall of man as described in the book of

Genesis. First God's spirit, in the form of a dove, broods over chaos, but out of this chaos we see God creating man, taking from him a rib and with this creating man's companion Eve. Next God, accompanied by his angels, warns the two never to eat fruit from the tree of knowledge, around which is already coiled the evil serpent. The serpent tempts Eve to take some fruit for herself and to offer one to her husband. So they fall, and are driven out of paradise on earth. This lost Garden of Eden is now shown surrounded by fire, to keep out humankind. The two fallen ones are forced to work for a living. Sin has come into the world. Next their sons are seen quarrelling over which sacrifice – Cain's corn or Abel's lamb – is more acceptable to God, and Cain in a rage murders Abel. Finally this pillar carries a sweet rustic scene of sheep-breeding and farming.

Every episode in this story is framed by a branch of ivy, which curls its way from the bottom of the pillar. In the second pillar the scenes are framed by the branches of an acanthus tree. The episodes range from the story of the Jewish patriarch Abraham to the prophecies of the birth of Jesus, ending with an angel flying to the Virgin Mary with the good news that she is to conceive the Son of God.

Pillar three recounts the life of Jesus, from his birth to his resurrection from death. The last pillar tells of our own fate, some of us consigned to hell after we rise from the dead, others led by angels to paradise, all of us judged by Christ who, in the fifth panel, sits in judgment. To match the first two sets of reliefs, in these last two the various scenes are again separated, first by the branches of an acanthus and, second, by a vine.

Step back again, after examining these delicate reliefs, to admire the whole façade again and note the cornice which runs above the reliefs along the entire front. For this Maitani sculpted and cast four bronzes, the symbols of the four evangelists, Matthew, Mark, Luke and John. At the same height, for the lintel of the main doorway, Maitani created a canopy held by angels, which houses – though one can scarcely see it – a 'Madonna and Child' sculpted by Andrea Pisano in 1347.

By contrast with these reliefs, the bronze doors of Orvieto cathedral seem to me a disappointment. The Sicilian sculptor Emilio Greco created them in 1964, and the panels of the central one illustrate the seven works of mercy. One such work is to visit those in prison, and the man depicted so doing is Pope John XXIII, the first Pope for centuries to do such a thing.

Orvieto cathedral continued to attract outstanding architects after Maitani's death in 1330, and the rose window was created between 1354 and 1380 by the Florentine Andrea di Cione, who is better known as Orcagna. At the very centre he sculpted the head of Jesus.

The cathedral is dedicated to the Virgin Mary in her Assumption, and most of the mosaics of the west façade, which date from the fourteenth to the nineteenth century, relate to her life. Inside, too, we are constantly reminded of her presence, for instance in the fourteenth-century frescos in the apse and above all in a lovely, though slightly tarnished, fresco of the 'Madonna and Child' which Gentile da Fabriano painted in 1425. You will find it on the wall to the left of the main entrance, just by the font. I try to ignore the figure of St Catherine on the right, which Giovambattista Ragazzini of Ravenna presumed to add in 1586.

Already we have seen Gentile's 'Madonna and Child' in the Umbrian National Gallery in Perugia. In that painting the artist's desire to produce a naturalistic, even agitated scheme for the Virgin Mary's dress is so much at odds with the Gothic style that he inherited that the tension gives the work an extraordinary power.

Gentile da Fabriano, though born in the Marches around 1370, was trained in Lombardy, and he clearly loved the Lombard books of illuminations whose elegance he magnified in his own frescos. At the same time, again and again in his paintings you can see him striving to express what a woman's dress looks like when its folds are determined by their linings. Sometimes he paints a Mary Magdalen whose dress billows to reveal the lining itself.

He moved from Lombardy to Venice, decisively influencing artists of the calibre of Jacopo Bellini and Pisanello. At this time too he took to painting those who people his pictures with fuller, gentler faces. All these elements he brought to bear on his Madonna in Orvieto cathedral. The Virgin and the child both gleam with plump health. Mary's dark-blue mantle parts to reveal a green lining (you can even see its red stitching), and the folds of her dress fall agitatedly to the ground. The realism of this fresco represents the highest peak of Gentile's art. Two years later he was dead.

The font near his 'Madonna and Child' is a different sort of masterpiece, created sixty-five years later by Luca di Giovanni (who also made the octagonal base) and added to by Sano di Matteo (who designed the Gothic temple on top, on which perches John the Baptist). Further down is a still more exotic holy water stoup designed by the exuberant Ippolito Scalza. But these details are not what first astounds one inside Orvieto cathedral. The overwhelming impression is one of spatial peace, white and green bands of stone complementing the colours outside. Then your eye begins to make out the richly carved and varied capitals.

The apse frescos, though several times restored (once by no less a master than Pintoricchio), exude the authentic aura of fourteenth-century Orvietan spirituality. Maitani himself supervised much of the creation of the stained glass which enhances the slender east window. He probably also designed the intricate choir stalls which a Siennese master, Giovanni Ammannati, made in 1329.

This intricacy pales beside the flamboyance of two works by Ippolito Scalza: a carved *pietà* and the massive organ case. For the *pietà* one could almost imagine that Scalza had decided to outmatch Gentile da Fabriano's skill at re-creating swirling drapery, so wildly does the carving flow. I find it immensely impressive that the whole, including the ladder and the old man with pincers and a hammer, was sculpted out of a single block of marble. As for the organ case, it now houses an instrument bigger than even Ippolito Scalza envisaged, for at the last restoration in 1975 another 1,585 pipes were added to its original 4,000.

This organ is situated in the left transept where you enter the chapel of the Holy Corporal, named after the very piece of altar linen which soaked up the blood from the sacred Host in 1263. Twice a year, on Easter Day and on the Feast of Corpus Christi, you can see the corporal itself, though probably only over the top of other people's heads. On these two feast days the relic is paraded through every quarter of the city, accompanied by 300 citizens dressed in medieval costume representing knights, magistrates, captains, standard-bearers and long-dead noble families. The players of Orvieto clearly relish such occasions, for on the Feast of the Assumption (14 August) once again they dress up, this time parading through the streets with the statue of Maria Assunta from the church of Sant'Andrea.

Do not neglect to visit the chapel at other times of the year, for the sacred relic is contained in a superb silver-gilt reliquary made by Ugolino di Vieri in the late 1330s. He was inspired enough to model it on Maitani's cathedral façade, and added enamel panels recounting the miracle of Bolsena. Two Orvietan artists decorated this chapel with frescos also depicting the miracle. These are fine enough, but nothing like as great as another painting in the chapel, Lippo Memmi's 'Madonna of Mercy'. Our Lady sweetly prays, while relieved mortals shelter under her blue robe. Finally, Orcagna added to the riches of this chapel by designing its marble tabernacle.

The opposite transept of the cathedral is even more extraordinary and entrancing. Built at the very end of the fourteenth century as the New Chapel and now called the Capella della Madonna di San Brizio, after a miracle-working statue of the Madonna had been placed here, it was initially frescoed in part by Fra Angelico and Benozzo Gozzoli. The cathedral authorities of Orvieto meditated long about whom they might commission to complete the work and finally made the inspired choice of Luca Signorelli.

Born in Cortona in the mid-fifteenth century, Signorelli had already worked in the Umbrian city of Città di Castello. Ten years later, in 1484, he was working on the San Onofrio altarpiece for the cathedral of Perugia. As his work matured he was not only absorbing the techniques which his master Piero della Francesca had learnt from the brilliant Florentines of the age. He was also mastering the remarkable skills at depicting the play of human muscle under strain developed by the Florentine genius Antonio Pollaiuolo. All this can be seen in his frescos in the Capella di San Brizio – and more, for in spite of these influences Luca Signorelli remained his own man, relishing the bodily beauty of his subjects, giving them a physicality you can almost touch.

On 5 April 1499 Signorelli was commissioned to begin work on the vaults of this chapel. Fra Angelico and Benozzo Gozzoli had finished only two sections, the one depicting Christ as judge of the earth, sitting on the clouds of heaven, and a scene of prophets singing his glory (you can recognize it by the words PROPHETARVM LAVDABILIS NVMERVS). Signorelli did the rest. It is a testimony to his sensitivity that he reined in his own exuberance in order not to destroy the symmetry begun by his two predecessors fifty years earlier. Yet the brilliance of his maturity bursts from the surface of everything he painted here. I find it a fascinating exercise to compare his fresco of the doctors of the Church (entitled DOCTORVM SAPIENS ORDO) with the earlier fresco of the prophets. Signorelli's doctors are far more richly coloured. Each one is individually realized, their gestures distinct, their poses varied, the whole powerful mass of men none the less superbly controlled.

The superintendents of the cathedral works were clearly impressed and on 27 April the following year they asked Signorelli to fresco the walls of the chapel as well. The project inspired him to produce a work almost unmatched in scope in the early Renaissance: a series of panels depicting aspects of the Last Judgment. He seized on the opportunity to exploit human nakedness in depicting the resurrection, the chosen ones and the damned. In his fresco of the joy of the saved he choicely contrasted the virile and succulent male and female bodies with the fully clothed angels which he painted above them (for, as Scripture tells us, angels have neither passions nor parts).

When he came to paint the damned – again a cornucopia of buttocks, twisting muscles and breasts – Signorelli could not resist including several naked devils as well as painting three lordly angels (fully armed to keep the wicked out of heaven). Now Pollaiuolo's pioneering experiments in painting tortured human anatomy reaches an eerie perfection in Signorelli's fresco, as the damned strain in anguish, some of them vainly trying to beat off or escape their captors.

Even when painting scenes from the end of the world on the arch at the entrance to the Capella di San Brizio, the muscles of Signorelli's fully clothed men and women flex and strain. Finally he included in this spectacular sequence of frescos a most unusual panel: the stories of the Antichrist. In the centre is a person who resembles Jesus (though on closer inspection his face is evil, and what he is preaching is being whispered in his ear by a horned devil). The scene takes place in Jerusalem, as we can tell from the temple in the background. To its left the Antichrist is being vigorously thrown out of heaven by the Archangel Gabriel. Below this scene a number of unfortunates are being slaughtered. In the left foreground is the most delightful detail of the whole series. Just beside a man who is being strangled to death two men in black robes walk nonchalantly by. The one who looks out at us, his hair falling expressively from his hat, is a self-portrait of Luca Signorelli himself. The man behind has short hair, his tonsure hidden by his skull-cap. Beneath his black cloak you can see the robe of a Dominican. Signorelli is paying tribute to the genius who worked on this chapel before him, Fra Angelico. Presumably he thought Gozzoli not worth a mention.

For this whole work the virtuoso was paid 575 ducats. We know he asked for it to be partly commuted to payments in kind, including a house with two beds, two monthly bushels of wheat and 125 litres of wine a year.

Such an overwhelming artistic experience is perhaps all that a normal visitor needs for one day, so maybe it is best to save for another time a visit to the cathedral museum, which stands down the steps on the south side. It used to be called the Palace of the Popes, and was built at the end of the thirteenth and in the first half of the fourteenth centuries: a simple building, the colour of the tufa which created its stones, rising above a powerful colonnade and reached by an outside staircase. Beyond it stands another of Orvieto's grand palaces, this one the Palazzo Buzi which Ippolito Scalza built around 1580.

A glass of wine, or a coffee and a cake, are happily on offer in the cafés and restaurants on the other side of the cathedral, dominated by the Torre di Maurizio. (Maurizio was the name of the founder who, in 1351, cast the bells on top of this tower, as well as the man in his peaked hat who rings them.) If you need a meal and you enjoy quails, search the menu for *quaglie rincartate*, for the chefs of Orvieto have their own way of cooking these delicate birds in dough.

Oddly enough I have sometimes found it impossible to buy the celebrated DOC wine of Orvieto itself in the bars and trattorie of the city, which is a great pity for this drink has been cultivated here since the days of the Etruscans. To determine the precise composition of its grapes demands such a long tradition, I think, for a judicious mixture of no fewer than five varieties (Scchetto, Verdello, Drupeggio, Malvasia Toscana and Trebbiano Toscana) is called for in producing either the dry *secco* or the sweet *abboccato*, both of which are extremely useful on a hot day (or on a cold day, for that matter).

Refreshed, with Orvieto or if necessary some other white, take the narrow Via Maitani opposite the west façade of the cathedral. The first palace on the right is the mighty Palazzo

Faina, housing an archaeological museum packed with many of the Etruscan treasures that have been recovered from the region. It opens from April to October from 09.00 to 13.00 and from 15.30 to 18.00, but outside the tourist season its curators take an hour less for lunch but close an hour and a half earlier in the evening.

Shortly the picturesque Renaissance street reaches on the left the church of San Francesco, which consists of a very satisfying classical interior inside a thirteenth-century skin. You enter by a doorway whose elegance derives from the fact that its decoration is sparse and all the more effective for it. A dove representing the Holy Spirit descends on us from the middle of the dome. Either Lorenzo Maitani himself, or one of his pupils, created the crucifix in wood over the high altar. In the thirteenth century this church was chosen for the funeral service of a nephew of King Henry III of England. It was conducted by Pope Gregory X after the unfortunate prince had been assassinated by the son of Simon de Montfort, enraged at his own father's death while fighting the troops of Henry III at the battle of Evesham. Here you can savour the brick and stone arches of the cloisters which Ippolito Scalza designed and which now serve as Orvieto's school of art, technology and commerce.

Walk south from the church down Via Ippolito Scalza, and bearing right you reach the pale brown stones of the church of San Lorenzo dé Arari. Built between the thirteenth and fifteenth centuries, it encompasses simple, plastered round pillars and on the west wall a busy fresco of St Lawrence himself – saving souls who skip happily into his arms, helping the poor, lame and sick, being arraigned before a king and finally martyred on a griddle. Note the sly torturer who puffs at the flames with a pair of bellows.

The pattern of streets of Orvieto has here suddenly become quirkily ancient. Via Maffati leads on the north side of San Francesco, with private houses let into the wall. Take the second street on the right, through an arch to the square in which stands San Francesco, turn immediately left and there rises the balcony of the Palazzo Mondaldeschi, now the Umbrian state art institute. If you take the road on the left of this building, Via Beato Angelico leads to a much more impressive palace, dating from the 1560s. Once again the architect was the vivacious Ippolito Scalza. His palace today houses the city library. Scalza was evidently fond of cockleshells as decoration, and huge ones embellish the architraves of his windows.

From here take another zigzag route, turning left at the end of the piazza into Via Cipriano Manente, immediately left again and instantly right. In a moment you will see the warm, brown twelve-sided and battlemented campanile of the church of Sant'Andrea. To reach it pass through an archway at the end of the street, which quaintly connects with a second one leading right into a graciously spacious piazza. This is the Piazza della Repubblica, where you will now no doubt judge that earlier I was foolish to suggest that we should not initially linger but should press on to the cathedral.

Sant'Andrea's Romanesque campanile has three rows of double-arched lights to let out the sound of its bells, and is decorated with ecclesiastical coats of arms carved from stone. The Gothic doorway of the church itself dates from the fourteenth century, and the 'Madonna and Child' in its lunette is the work of Paoli Pogiliani, sculpted in 1928. Abutting the church rises the Palazzo Communale, another of Scalza's grandiose architectural gifts to Orvieto.

At the opposite end of the piazza from the church of Sant'Andrea begins a medieval quarter of Orvieto which has been dubbed the 'Quartiere del'Olmo' – the elm quarter. It is part of the city to wander in at will, housing crumbling palaces and ancient churches, flanked by mouldering walls, offering occasional splendid views of the surrounding countryside, little visited by the tourist and enlivened by children playing in the street. But I warn you, in most of these streets there is not a bar in sight.

Often you can buy flowers from stalls at the south side of

Sant'Andrea, from which leads Corso Cavour (which does contain its proper quota of bars). When you reach the Torre del Moro, take the second left and walk along between the shops of Via San Lorenzo to find the complex, yet entirely satisfying, Palazzo del Capitano del Popolo. Pope Hadrian IV inaugurated the building of this lovely half-Romanesque, half-Gothic palace in 1157. I do not know which Pope gave it to the commune of Orvieto, but I could never have been so generous. The Orvietans then added to the building another large hall and the belfry at the east end. What might have seemed a dour defensive palace is lightened by the delicately mullioned windows. In one of them is carved the cheeky head of a grinning man.

Opposite the Palazzo del Capitano del Popolo rises the Romanesque church of San Rocco. If you want to see more frescos, in 1527 Cristoforo da Marciano decorated the apse with Jesus and his mother, along with Saints Roch, Sebastian and John the Baptist. The other sixteenth-century fresco, of the 'Madonna and Child' with four saints, is by Eusebio da Montefiascone. Adding to the riches of this piazza is a nineteenth-century palazzo by the Roman architect Virginio Vespignani. It now serves as a luxury hotel.

The Piazza del Popolo is the largest square in Orvieto and plays host each Thursday and Saturday morning to a market whose stalls are shaded by colourful awnings. Stroll by the right-hand side of the Palazzo del Capitano del Popolo and find Via Corsica, turning right along it into the Via della Pace to reach Piazza XXIX Marzio and the church of San Domenico. Shaded by sycamores and pine trees, this piazza is dedicated to the memory of seven sons of Orvieto who were assassinated by Fascists on 29 March 1944 for their part in the Italian resistance in World War II.

The contrast between the grey and white striped square pillars, some of them still partly unfaced, and the tufa between them makes you think of a combination of ice-cream and golden-brown syrup. The interior of the church comes as a tremendous surprise, for its dimensions seem to run the wrong way round. San Domenico is four times as broad as it is long. It houses many treasures, of which two are of outstanding interest, though for different reasons. One is on the left of the entrance, a monument to a Frenchman, Cardinal de Braye, which Arnolfo di Cambio created in 1282. The other is a chair. It is lovingly preserved in a showcase to the left of the altar, for this was the chair from which St Thomas Aquinas taught. Aquinas was staying in the sadly demolished Dominican monastery attached to this church in 1263 when the Host raised by Friar Peter of Prague dripped blood on to the corporal, and here he wrote his 'Pange lingua'. From the square in which this Dominican church stands a sign points back down Via Felice Cavaletti to the cathedral which was built in the miracle's honour.

So rich is the heritage of Orvieto that this tour has certainly not visited every architectural treasure. The churches of San Giovanni and Santa Maria dei Servi, the one built in the fifteenth and sixteenth centuries, the other a neat example of Virginio Vespignani's mid-nineteenth-century classical style, both contain beautiful works of art. If you find yourself in Via Malabranca, make your way into the courtyard of no. 22, the early Renaissance Palazzo Michelangeli, and gasp at the elegance of its arcades and loggia.

The surrounding countryside is equally richly sown with gems of villages and towns, and not far away is one of Umbria's most stunning hill cities, Todi. To savour these delights take the Via Postierla, which leads from the cathedral north-east to the papal Rocca, from where you drive down to the suburb of Orvieto Scalo. Here are the remains of an Etruscan temple on your right and signs pointing left up towards the Etruscan tombs, an eerie city of the dead known as the Croce del Tufo.

The hilly, scenic route soon offers an impressive view of old Baschi. Over to the left is the artificial lake of Corbara, a huge shimmering reservoir created by damming the Tiber. It can accommodate 137 million cubic metres of water, and is a haven for fishermen, whose catches are sold in the restaurants and grilled in the campsites that ring its shores. If you make a detour to Lago di Corbara, don't miss the medieval ambience of the village of Castello di Lago.

Baschi stands on a 165-metre-high spur, and has laudably supplemented the attractions of its medieval self by catering for sports enthusiasts. The parish church of San Nicolò dates from the fifteenth century, but Ippolito Scalza came here and matched, on a smaller scale, his achievement at Orvieto cathedral by adding a façade in the late 1570s. If the church is open, make sure you see a triptych in the south transept painted by Giovanni di Paolo around 1440.

For a moment or two the road runs south-east alongside the Autostrada del Sole and then follows the gentle Tiber to Lago di Alviano. In 1978 the Umbrians declared this lake and its surrounding countryside a protected oasis. The rich marshland is ideal soil for willows, poplars and alders. The sedges and reeds, the bulrushes and little scrublands have become a haven for migrating birds. Herons and reed-warblers, bitterns and water hens abound. Falcons, sandpipers and remarkable varieties of duck – eighty different species in all – live and mate here. Cormorants and wild geese pause on their journeys back and forth during their biennial migrations. Late autumn and early spring are the seasons when ornithologists flock to the seven observatories already installed in the oasis for that most satisfying and peaceful pursuit, birdwatching. Other visitors indulge in the mildest of sports in which a creature is actually caught and killed: fishing – for eel, catfish, carp and luce in the lake, the streams that water the oasis and the Tiber itself.

The whole district has become a natural paradise. At Alviano the ilex wood has been equipped with well-serviced picnic spots. To cater for the diverse tastes of the tourist, the town of Guardea boasts not only a forest of ilex and pines, which shelter red deer, but also tennis courts and a roller-skating rink that overlooks the lake. The charming hill towns and villages in and around this oasis are constantly beguiling

1 *The mighty* rocca *and the Ponte della Torri of Spoleto were both designed by Matteio Gattapone in the mid-fourteenth century.*

2 *Castelluccio – one of the countless hilltop towns which dot Umbria.*

3 *The west façade of the cathedral at Orvieto, glinting in the sun and rising from a stupendous outcrop of volcanic rock.*

4 (Opposite above) *Looking down from the Piazza della Signoria over the medieval rooftops of Gubbio.*

5 (Opposite below) *Each morning the steep steps which lead down from the centre of Perugia are crammed with colourful market stalls.*

6 (Overleaf) *Luca Signorelli's frescos for the chapel of the Madonna of S. Brizio in Orvieto cathedral. The man in black* (foreground right), *apparently oblivious to what is going on, is a self-portrait of the artist himself.*

7 *Todi beckons in the distance, a town that has stood here since Etruscan times.*

8 (Opposite above) *The towering basilica and convent of San Francesco, Assisi, consecrated by Pope Innocent IV in 1253.*

9 (Opposite below) *Ancient belltowers rising above the fortified city of Narni.*

10 *Maize dries peacefully in the sun beside an Umbrian farm.*

and some of them have been here for centuries, witness the Etruscan tombs and prehistoric remains at Montécchio, north of Guardea. All of this peaceful area is genially overseen by the local tourist board in the municipality of Alviano (tel. 0744 904110).

Alviano itself, nine kilometres east of the lake, is ancient enough once to have belonged to a branch of the family of the Roman historian Livy. As you drive into the town its severe fourteenth-century Castello warns you not to take liberties. It was here that St Francis, preaching in 1212, ordered all the swallows to stop their twittering so that the people could hear his sermon. (The event is depicted in a sixteenth-century fresco in the chapel of the Castello.) Both Giovanni de' Sacchis da Pordenone and Nicolò Alunno helped to decorate the fourteenth-century parish church of this medieval town, the latter contributing a finely restrained fresco of the Madonna in glory.

Lugnano in Teverina lies by a winding, undulating route a few kilometres south-east of Alviano and boasts its own pine forest replete with children's playgrounds and picnic spots. Drive up to park in Piazza Umberto I, in which stands the twelfth-century church of Santa Maria Assunta, a perfect example of Umbrian Romanesque architecture. The symbols of the four evangelists over the porch, though simple, are equally as moving as those on the west façade of Orvieto cathedral. Inside, eight massive round pillars, some with patterned capitals, some with capitals decorated with human beings, lead you to the east end and the entrance to the Romanesque crypt, again supported on eight round pillars though this time extremely slender ones. Climb up to the altar above, which is still sheltered by a Romanesque *baldacchino*. The severe pulpit is none the less beautifully decorated and the pavement is an ancient mosaic.

Lugnano in Teverina is one of those places that make you realize how the medieval Christians built far more churches than they could ever fill with worshippers. The campanile of Santa Maria Assunta actually abuts on to another one.

Opposite is the municipal tourist office, in a medieval palazzo. Over the medieval walls of the town appear more of those green vistas for which Umbria is famed. Alleyways and steep, arched passages lead by houses with flower-decked balconies to yet more churches.

Feeling hungry there one evening around six o'clock, I just managed to make it to the bakery and cake shop in Via Cavour before closing time. If you are there with enough daylight left, on leaving Lugnano in Teverina take the sign for Attigliano, which lies ten kilometres south-west. The road passes the convent of San Francesco, built in 1229 on the spot where St Francis quelled the noisy swallows. Delightfully situated on the edge of a plain overlooking the Tiber, medieval Attigliano has preserved the walls of its former castle, and its inhabitants (of whom there are scarcely more than 2,000) when not farming devote themselves to producing ceramics and wrought-iron. The road runs on south-east, crossing a little tributary of the Tiber, and then snakes east up to an even tinier village, Giove, five and a half kilometres away, whose crumbling walls and medieval heart are charming.

Just over twelve kilometres north-east from Giove, by a picturesquely twisting road, lies Amélia, a citadel set on a hill between the Rivers Tiber and Nera. In Roman times Amélia was important enough to be mentioned by Cato. A stronghold against the barbarian invasions, it was virtually destroyed by the Goths in 548. During the Middle Ages the commune rose again under the sway of the Church, though frequently pillaged and sacked by the warring factions of the time (Barbarossa was one who besieged her). Amélia suffered once again in 1832 from a severe earthquake. Yet she remains exquisite, her massive polygonal walls, dating from the fifth century BC, excluding the slightly nondescript modern town that has grown up around them. The rude powerful Roman blocks support a clearly distinguishable medieval superstructure.

Park outside its elaborate classical gateway, which is

topped by a brick one from which branches grow. Through the gateway rises a narrow street bordered at first by elegant fashion shops, jewellers and a shop selling fine glassware. A sign of Amélia's increasing prosperity after the ravages of the Middle Ages is that the Romanesque church here has been given a classical interior. But as you climb (and you *do* climb), you soon realize that you are in an unspoilt medieval and Renaissance hill town, with cobblers and woodworkers replacing the fashionable shops further down the street. Curving steps lead off into dark cosy alleyways. The fourteenth-century church of Sant'Agostino (with a rich Gothic façade of 1477) is well-scrubbed, and one Tuesday evening when I went in for Mass I found it packed. As I was late and missed the collect, I can't say which saint's day we were celebrating, but the date was 11 November.

Take the signs not for the Duomo but for the Porta Romana, to reach – through an archway – the entrancing Piazza Marconi, with the proud seventeenth-century Palazzo Petricignani standing next to the crumbling sixteenth-century Palazzo Naci. Steps between them lead to the curving, steep route on the right which reaches the surprisingly huge classical cathedral, with its ancient twelve-sided campanile. This dates from 1050 and incorporates stones from an even earlier, Roman tower. The cathedral was also once Romanesque, but was completely rebuilt in 1640. In one of its chapels (the second on the right) there are a couple of Turkish standards captured at the Battle of Lepanto. If you have developed a taste for the decidedly unreserved architecture of Ippolito Scalza, look for the tombs of Baldo and Bartolomeo Farrattini.

Narni is twelve kilometres south-east, reached by a road which passes by way of Fórnole and the San Silvestro park and situated on a limestone rock 240 metres above sea-level, overlooking both the Terni plain and the River Nera from which, in Roman times, it derived its name. Narni itself is dominated by the still-powerful ruins of its Rocca, built by Cardinal Albornoz around 1370 to keep the independent-minded citizens loyal to the Church. They had rebelled against papal rule in 1122, and later managed to keep themselves out of the clutches of both Frederick Barbarossa and Frederick II.

St Francis not only preached here but is said to have performed a good number of miracles too. He certainly founded a convent here in 1213, though the church of San Francesco presently on the spot was built in the fourteenth century. The fresco of the 'Madonna and Child' over the Gothic entrance was painted in the seventeenth century, and inside are some earlier ones dating from the fourteenth and fifteenth centuries.

Christianity had been brought here long before, by St Giovenale who became bishop of the city in the year 369. To him Narni cathedral is dedicated, a Romanesque building consecrated in 1145 and much restored and altered since. Yet the interior has managed to retain its ancient aspect, with three naves separated by simple low columns and a polygonal apse. A fourth nave on the right was added in the fourteenth century. Narni cathedral houses many treasures, not least the inlaid choir stalls of 1490 and a pulpit of the same date, bearing finely carved saints. Although it was rebuilt in the fifteenth and sixteenth centuries by masons who re-used the Romanesque materials, the mortuary chapel (the *sacello*) contains the oldest surviving elements of Narni's first cathedral, including a delicate sixth-century marble altar and the seventh-century sandstone coffin in which St Giovenale still lies.

Leave the cathedral by its south door and walk down the steps into Piazza Garibaldi, which used to be called the piazza of the lake because the main city fountain is here. In this square another medieval belfry, now a clock-tower, vies with the cathedral campanile. The cathedral square itself is dedicated to Cavour, another patriot of the Italian Risorgimento, and from it the shady Via Garibaldi, the awnings of whose shops and bars offer yet more shade, leads to the secular centre of the city, the entrancing Piazza dei Priori.

The priors' own palace has a vast loggia supported on a central pillar which most scholars think can have been designed only by that astonishing mid-fourteenth-century architect Matteo Gattapone. It faces another remarkable building, the Palazzo del Podestà, created in the fifteenth century out of three thirteenth-century buildings, each with its own tower. Today it is the city art gallery, displaying (on the first floor) a gorgeous 'Coronation of the Virgin' by Domenico Ghirlandaio and a vivid fresco by Giovanni Spagna of St Francis receiving the stigmata.

Before you go in, don't miss over the right of the doorway four quaint thirteenth-century bas-reliefs. They depict a lion and a dragon, a hunting scene (with a hawk), two knights duelling and the beheading of Holofernes.

Narni also has an ecclesiastical museum, in the former Dominican church, a Romanesque building which you reach by the continuation of Via Garibaldi, dedicated to a third hero of the Risorgimento, Mazzini. On the way you pass the pretty little church of Santa Maria in Pensole, which was built in 1175.

Twelve or so kilometres north-east of Narni the River Nera is joined by the Serra, and the Romans named the town here 'between two rivers', or Interamna, which today has become Terni. Terni suffered considerable bombing in World War II and today suffers from industrial sprawl, but if you seek you will find some treasures, including the remains of its first-century AD amphitheatre. Tacitus was born here and from the modern piazza dedicated to him rise the waters of a post-war fountain enlivened with pretty mosaics. Corso Cornelio Tacito leads from here to Piazza della Repubblica, whose graceless town hall was built by Benedetto Faustini in 1878 and unfortunately survived the war.

Via Cavour, which runs from the right side of this piazza, has more to interest the lover of Umbria's past, for the first house is recognizably Gothic and no. 14 is the Palazzo Mastrozzi, built by Antonio Sangallo the Younger in the early sixteenth century. Terni has restored the medieval Palazzo dei Mazzancolli at no. 28 as its municipal art gallery, and the sweet courtyard with its double loggia and staircase is well worth a visit itself.

Return along Via Cavour and turn right into Piazza Europa, at the far end of which is another of Sangallo the Younger's works, the Palazzo Spada. Behind this is a comical gem, the church of San Salvatore. Built on the site of a Roman temple dedicated to the sun god, this twelfth-century church is in two parts, one cylindrical, one square.

Via Roma continues from Piazza Europa, passing (at nos 54 and 56) the seventeenth-century Palazzo Pierfelici and reaching on the right Via dell'Arrenga, which takes you to the cathedral. A modern fountain plays in the Piazza del Duomo, and the two cathedral doorways, one Romanesque, the other fourteenth-century Gothic, scarcely prepare you for the fact that most of the rest of the building dates from the sixteenth and seventeenth centuries, or even later. Terni cathedral was reconsecrated in 1653 and its campanile rebuilt in 1743. Even the crypt, where St Anastasius lies, was overmodernized in the twentieth century. But I do like the baroque organ of Terni cathedral, built by Luca Neri in 1647, and though I cannot say I also like the grandiose altar and tabernacle of 1762, I admit to being impressed by its sheer pomp.

As you leave the cathedral by its main doors, you spot across the piazza the Palazzo Bianchini-Riccardi, said to be by the pupils of Antonio da Sangallo the Younger. To find Sant'Alò, an excellently restored eleventh-century Roman-esque church (which is usually locked), take Via 11 Febbraio at the north side of the piazza and turn left into Via Sant'Alò. Its name is a corruption of St Aloysius.

The one church that should not be missed in Terni is San Francesco, which you find by walking back to Via 11 Feb-braio from Sant'Alò and turning left along Via Antonio Fratti. Begun in 1265 by Franciscans who remembered that in Terni cathedral their founder had thanked the bishop for describ-ing him as a worthless wretch, the campanile was enriched by the Gothic architect Angelo da Orvieto in 1345. The apse dates from exactly 100 years later and is lovely. Left of the nave is the so-called paradise chapel (Capella Paradisi), built in the fourteenth century and frescoed in the next century with scenes from Dante's *Divine Comedy*. Since these include scenes from hell, purgatory and limbo as well as paradise, the name seems initially odd. It derives in fact from the name of the artists, Angelo and Paolo Paradisi. On the south side of the church a couple of mighty round pillars are leaning perilously outwards – but a man leaning his bicycle against one of them told me that they have been so for centuries without falling down.

In spite of these occasional treats Terni is, to my mind, more a place for excursions than for prolonged examination. The most exciting excursion is to the celebrated Marmore Falls (the Cascata delle Marmore), a dozen kilometres south-east of the city (reached by route 79, keeping your eyes open for the turning off to the left). The Romans created these exquisite waterfalls, which tumble 165 metres over three great rocks, when they diverted the River Velino to drain the marshy plain above. Since today the falls have been harnessed to produce hydroelectricity, they can be seen only on Sundays and feast days. The authorities sometimes make up for this deprivation by illuminating them in childish colours.

If you continue along route 79, thirteen kilometres from Terni you reach another beauty spot, the peaceful village of Piediluco, situated on a lake which bears its name (it means 'at the foot of the forest'). Piediluco has a Romanesque church dedicated to St Francis, and its lake is surrounded by beaches and tranquil campsites, all guarded by the remains of another of those fortresses which Cardinal Albornoz built to keep the Umbrians in order, this one peering down from the top of a conical hill. The lake has an echo that delights children, and lovers – whom it prompts to behave like children.

Small wonder that Terni mounts an annual festival of water in June. On 30 April the citizens also tour the city with decorated floats during the 'Cantamaggio' celebrations. And the city hosts an international piano competition in May.

To reach Todi from Terni, drive north-west along route 79 to call first at San Gémini. Half-modern, half-medieval, this picturesque spot was noted by the Romans for its thermal spring (which is still as therapeutic as ever, though more people take the waters these days at nearby San Gémini Fonte), and a Roman mosaic has been discovered in the city centre. In Piazza Vecchio the seventeenth-century Palazzo del Popolo is entered by way of an arcaded external staircase. Next to it is an oratory with some restrained, but moving, fifteenth-century frescos.

This is by no means the only church of note in San Gémini. San Francesco, begun in the thirteenth and finished in the fourteenth century, has a splendid Gothic doorway whose wooden door is probably the original one. Inside, the church is graced with ogival arches. San Giovanni, founded in 1199, has an impressive Romanesque porch.

In San Gémini there is a curiosity: a thirteenth-century church dedicated to San Nicolò which is not only private property but has a reproduction porch, since the original is now on display in the Metropolitan Museum, New York. A fresco inside dated 1295 is the only surviving work of Master Rogerino da Todi. And one of its pillars, the first one on the left, is certainly Roman in origin. It came from nearby Carsulae (three kilometres north-east through San Gémini Fonte and across the main road), a magical Roman find, with its amphitheatre and theatre, long ago a station on the old Flaminian Way.

Drive on north to Acquasparta, whose name indicates that as far back as Roman times its waters were of great repute. Maybe the Romans drank them while driving their chariots just as, to avoid dangerous driving, I sip mineral water when touring by car. These waters do vary. One I bought at San Girgio not far from Cascia was so sharp (*frizzante* said the label, but that only means sparkling) that at the next stop I threw it away. Another moot point is whether they are quite

as effective as their labels sometimes claim. Take Oligo-
minerale Fonte Tullia (another *frizzante* water), which comes
from Spoleto. The label proclaims in English, Italian and
German: 'The Olige mineral water "Fonte Tullia" may have a
diuretic action and is suitable for diets poor in sodium.' By
my reckoning it sparkled like mad and really did taste of
sodium. On the other hand, I drank a whole bottle one day and
slept uninterruptedly throughout the night, which says little
for its diuretic effect. Obviously the word 'may' on the label
counts for a lot. As for the waters of Acquasparta itself, they
are said to be especially effective at curing gout, kidney
problems and arthritis.

Acquasparta bears its Roman past lightly. Its spectacular
Palazzo Cesi, which Giovanni Domenico Bianchi built in the
second half of the fifteenth century, now belongs to the
University of Perugia. Two churches are worth a call: the
late thirteenth-century San Francesco, with the remains of
its cloisters and its original altar; and Santa Cecilia, where
you will be delighted by a late sixteenth-century chapel.

On the way, if you have time, turn north-east at Rosceto to
see Massa Martana, for here there are Christian catacombs
next to a little third-century BC Roman bridge that crosses
the River Naia. Here too are some exquisite white stone
churches and abbeys (Santa Maria in Pantano, which is one
of Umbria's oldest, and Santa Maria delle Grazie). Beyond the
town Mount Martana rises to 1,094 metres. Don't miss the
isolated eleventh-century abbey of San Fidenzio and San
Terenzio, two or three kilometres north-west of Massa
Martana. A kilometre to the west stands another lovely
Romanesque church, Santa Illuminata.

To the west Todi perches high on its hill, its origins lost in
legend. Some say that Hercules founded it. Others say that a
man named Tudero and his companions, seeking a spot to
found a new home, sat down to eat at the foot of the hill when
an eagle swooped on them, snatched their tablecloth and
flew with it to the summit – a sure sign of a divine command
to build there. In plain truth, the origin of its name, the

Etruscan word *Tutere*, signifies a border town, and clearly
the Etruscans saw this site as strategically impregnable.
Traces of their defensive walls still remain. As you drive up to
the city, vineyards slope towards the sun and poppies dot the
fields of barley.

The most alluring way in is to wind your way up from the
south-west. Still outside the walls you pass the domed
church of Santa Maria delle Conzolatione, a beautiful
Renaissance building whose first builder was Cola da
Caprarola. The work was continued after his death in 1512 by
Ambroglio Barocci of Milan and Francesco da Vita. Their
efforts ended in 1524, but the dome was not added until 1607.
The whole is so impressive that some scholars insist that the
great Bramante himself designed the church.

Next on your left appears a little park, with a stunning
panorama. Drive on into the city through the Porta Orvetana
and past San Fortunato, which has no piazza. Its unfinished,
yet deeply satisfying Romanesque façade is approached by
some steps leading to a green lawn with scrupulously trim
patterned hedges. Turn left, glad still to be driving, for the
streets of Todi are steep, and you reach the great central
square of the city, the Piazzo del Popolo. The houses here are
both Gothic and Renaissance in style, each one a gem, most
of them built of the local limestone, sometimes embellished
with brick. Four of the buildings are outstanding. The grey-
brown, battlemented Palazzo dei Priori – three-storeyed and
with a battle-weary tower rising behind it – has occupied the
south side of the piazza since the beginning of the fourteenth
century. On the east side rises another battlemented palace,
the thirteenth-century Palazzo del Popolo, and next to it the
Gothic Palazzo del Capitano, built nearly eighty years later in
1290. A long flight of steps, over an arch, leads in front of this
palace to the Palazzo del Popolo, which now serves as one of
the city's art galleries.

At the opposite end of the square a sweep of steps rises to the
white stones, occasionally blushing pink, of the west façade
of Todi cathedral – Romanesque, with a decorated main

doorway that is just becoming Gothic. The cathedral was begun in the eleventh century and bears a delicate rose window above this main door, with two blank windows above the doors flanking it. The interior has retained its fine simplicity, allowing itself a hint of exuberance in the capitals and relaxing its austerity in the Gothic south aisle. A baroque organ at the east end throws caution to the winds.

People are at ease when they worship in the Duomo at Todi. I once discovered a choir of schoolchildren singing and attending Mass, which included the first Communion of six boys and two girls – the girls dressed in white like brides. When the Mass was over the whole congregation applauded the eight little Christians. Dominating it all was the twelfth- or thirteenth-century crucifix, painted on wood, with the hands of the dead Jesus alarmingly thin and elongated, the style Byzantine.

So far Todi has not greatly taxed our leg muscles, but it takes stamina to explore the city properly. On the east side of the Palazzo dei Priori is a most handsome fountain in its little piazza. Corso Cavour leads south from here, plunging into the narrow streets of medieval Todi. To the right a narrow flight of steps leads up under an almost flat arch supporting a house. On the left of Corso Cavour there next appears a little piazza with two lovely round arches guarding a medieval building behind a merry arcade. As you walk on, more steps lead steeply away up another street to the right.

Under an archway, Corso Cavour becomes the equally steep Via Roma. As you reach the narrow Via della Storia, which runs sharply down to the right, you spot signposts directing you to the Foro Romano and the church of San Ilario. Way down there the remains of the Roman theatre have been excavated; and San Ilario, consecrated in 1249, has a fresco by Giovanni Spagna depicting the Madonna del Soccorso.

Return from these jewels from Todi's past to continue along the Via Roma and turn right into Via Santa Maria in Communiccia. Antique houses press in on either side.

Glance down Vico di San Antonio, the first alleyway off to the right, to wonder at houses that would have long since tumbled in on each other but for buttresses straining to keep them apart. Then on the left a little square opens up to reveal the former Dominican monastery, which continues to rise massively beside you as you walk on. Churches, now seemingly unused, flank the street. You pass under a medieval arch to reach a second arch, known as the Porta Aurea. Someone must live in it, for a surprising window peers down from the upper part.

We are in the middle set of Todi's city walls. If you walk through the arch you are offered not only a panorama of the surrounding hills and valleys but also a glimpse of how the city, stepped downwards, has spread outside these walls. Retrace your steps back under the arch, and take the Via della Porta Libera, the winding, narrow, stepped street that leads up to the left. Towering above you is the spire of the church of San Fortunato, which you drove past as you entered Todi. Take the uphill route, a flight of overgrown steps that are simply set in the earth. This is not a climb for the disabled, the faint-hearted or the overweight. At the top, a ruined archway beckons you into the public park of the Piazza Oberdan, from which the marvellous vista includes an impressive view of the outer walls.

The way back to the centre of Todi takes us through the gateway with a house perched on top of it along the Via Lorenzo Leoni. Via di San Fortunato runs directly left to the church of San Fortunato, started in 1292. At last we can admire the exquisite Gothic doorway of its façade, the work of Giovanni di Santuccio from Firenzuola di Spoleto. The interior is a perfectly balanced Gothic whole, its nave and two aisles exactly matching each other in height.

By now we surely either need to sit down in this church or take a long beer outside, at the trattoria on the corner of Piazza Umberto I (where even the way to the *gabinetti* is up a flight of steps). Then Via Mazzini swings back into the cathedral square. Before we take it, note the modern statue of

Jacopone da Todi at the corner of Piazza Umberto I. Jacopone lies buried in the church of San Fortunato. This Franciscan mystic led his brethren in following the example of St Francis by composing praises to God and singing them up and down Umbria.

He and Francis perfectly complemented each other. On Christmas Eve 1223, St Francis had invited the local peasants at Greccio to an act of worship in his hermitage and produced for them the first ever Christmas crib – using live animals and a real child. Greccio is outside Umbria, but if you want to see an authentic fourteenth-century Christmas crib while staying within the boundaries of this province, visit Calvi dell'Umbria, thirty kilometres south of Terni on the border with Latium. Naturally, when Christmas comes the villagers re-enact the Nativity with a real baby and animals. Calvi dell'Umbria is ancient, built on a hill 401 metres above sea-level, and beyond it rises a range of oak and pine-clad mountains. A kilometre north of the village stands the convent which Francis himself founded in 1220.

The saint invented the Christmas crib, and his devout follower Jacopone wrote the first Italian Christmas carol:

> *Fiorito è Cristo nella carne pura:*
> *or se ralegri l'umana natura.*

(Christ has flowered in the pure flesh:
now let human nature rejoice.)

So passionately did Jacopone espouse poverty that Pope Boniface VIII excommunicated him for his vehemence. Happily, three years before Jacopone's death, Benedict XI absolved him. It seems a pity that such a good man should have been made to suffer in this way. But Jacopone had an answer. One of his hymns is entitled 'The greatest wisdom is to be considered mad for the love of Christ'. It begins:

> *Senno me pare e cortesia,*
> *empazir per lo bel Messia.*
> *Ello me sa si gran sapere*

> *a chi per Dio vol empazire,*
> *en Parige non se vidde*
> *ancor si gran filosofia.*

> (It seems to me to be sane and noble
> to go mad for the beautiful Messiah.
> To want to go mad for God
> seems to me great wisdom,
> no one has yet seen in Paris
> philosophy as great as this.)

Many entrancing excursions can be made from Todi. One takes you north-east to Collazzone, set on an olive-covered hill. The thirteenth-century church of San Ilario at Collazzone has a double-tiered open bell-tower. Jacopone died in this town in 1306 in the convent of San Lorenzo, which still stands. Inside the church of San Lorenzo is a poignant 'Madonna and Child', carved out of wood in the sixteenth century. The church's walls are fortified and turreted, with battlemented gates and houses let into them.

Another excursion is to Fratta Todina, eleven kilometres away, again massively fortified during the Middle Ages. Here Cardinal Altieri, Bishop of Todi, built himself a palace in the first half of the sixteenth century; Giovanni Santini designed the parish church in the next; and the Franciscans built themselves a convent outside the walls, whose eighteenth-century church survives today.

A third outing is north-west to Marsciano where, despite its commercial and industrial base, the medieval castle of Sant'Appolinare survives intact, the parish church houses a fresco by Perugino, and the tower and archway built by the medieval Bulgarelli clan still glower at you.

These are treats; but while at Todi I prefer to make an excursion that combines architectural, even spiritual refreshment with something for the stomach too. I had been told of a superb restaurant (and hotel too, for that matter) created from a thirteenth-century convent. Leaving Todi by the Porta Romana, I took the road to Ponte Naia, after that following the signs to Hotel San Valentino. The owner showed me around. Signor Agnello and his company bought the place when it was virtually a ruin, abandoned by the religious order; but today the Romanesque crypt is in perfect condition, and the apse of the church remains touchingly frescoed. He added that the hotel boasts a honeymoon suite with its own separate entrance, so that newly-weds are not disturbed by those whose first surge of love was experienced long ago and can scarcely be remembered now. At the time I did not think to ask him whether dedicating his hotel to St Valentine was his own invention, or whether the monks too had a special affection for the saint whose feast day is said to fall on the very day the birds mate.

Later I regretted this, for I should have liked to quote him a marriage song by our seventeenth-century English poet, and man of God too, about a couple married on St Valentine's Day. John Donne imagines people laying bets about which of the bridal pair will get up first, and spying on them to see who does – something impossible in the Hotel San Valentino, Todi:

> Others near you shall whispering speake,
> And wagers lay, at which side day will breake,
> And win by observing, then, whose hand it is
> That opens first a curtain, hers or his.

Our poet, to his credit, did expect the newly-weds to stay awake all night, and therefore extended St Valentine's Day to the following morning:

> This will be tryed to morrow after nine,
> To which houre, we thy day enlarge, O Valentine.

It was warm enough for me to eat on the terrace, overlooking the hotel swimming pool and across at Todi itself, rising above the valley, with Santa Maria della Consolazione high up to the left. If I regretted not quoting John Donne, I did not regret my meal, which began with slices of tomato and mushrooms, on top of which was laid mozzarella cheese made from the milk of Umbrian sheep. Next came home-made pasta, again a product for which Umbria is famous. This was not the coarser sort known as *strascinati*, but *umbricelli* served with salmon sauce and truffles. With the first course I had been sipping the white Grechetto di Todi, which was beautifully cold on this warm afternoon, but now I changed to a red Todi wine, Almonte Annata 1984, which had the scent of sweet olives. It matched the pudding of cream and cake. And as I downed my last glass of red wine, from a campanile in Todi the bells began to ring.

Spoleto, Norcia, Cascia and the hills

When you see the 672-foot-long bridge which the architect Matteo Gattapone built at Spoleto in the second half of the fourteenth century, you realize why his contemporaries thought him crazed as well as a genius. He built it on the base of a ruined Roman aqueduct. Today his bridge is known as the Ponte delle Torre. Frighteningly thin, narrow arches rise to a vertiginous height of 270 feet.

Drive or climb up Spoleto's twisting medieval streets to the very top of the city. Signposts alleviate the hair-raising panic provoked by the steep turns and the bulging corners which threaten to dent your car. They point to Rocca Albornoziana, to Ponte delle Torri and to the Hotel Gattapone. Once at the top you can park by the powerful castle (the Rocca) and look down over the steep cliffs on to Gattapone's astonishingly huge, yet slender, structure. You can walk along the narrow top ledge of the bridge, desperately resisting the urge to fling yourself to destruction over the side. Why has no Hitchcockian film-maker ever used the Ponte delle Torre for a spectacular murder or suicide?

I returned for a stiff drink at the discreetly modern Hotel

Gattapone, which seems itself to have been constructed tumbling down the cliffside. Building on the site of a seventeenth-century house, the architect had the foresight to design every one of its windows to overlook Gattapone's bridge. The slender arches look slightly safer from here and you notice that they lead across the deep cleft of the valley to a mini-Rocca on the opposite side.

Recovered and refreshed, now is the time to stroll downhill into the city past the Rocca Albornoziana. As you leave the hotel you can see over to the left the church of San Pietro, outside the city walls, and high on the hill a monastery. The Rocca too has a religious origin, though one would hardly guess this from its martial aspect. Once the haunt of Lucrezia Borgia, this massive fortress was also built by Gattapone, in 1359, for his patron, the papal legate Cardinal Albornoz. Each corner of his rectangular Rocca is guarded by a tower, and as if that were not enough to demonstrate that Albornoz was in earnest in reorganizing the papal states, two more towers rise from the centre of the longer walls. The largest of all glowers down on the city below.

It has served as a prison more than once. A notice on the wall records the pleasing fact that on 13 October and 26 November 1943 ninety-four Italians and Slovenians being held as political prisoners by the Fascists escaped from the Rocca into the nearby mountains to form the nucleus of the local anti-Mussolini partisans.

At the end of the Rocca a little flight of steps and then an archway lead down into Via Aurelia Saffi, on the right of which is the Piazza del Duomo of Spoleto. But before descending the wide flight of stairs that leads to the cathedral, walk a little further down the narrow street to reach the fifteenth-century Archbishops' Palace, which has been turned into the diocesan museum of religious art, a rich collection of works from the thirteenth century onwards.

The palace encloses in its courtyard a delicate, early twelfth-century gem, the church of Santa Eufemia. Pink bricks enliven its clean, unpretentious Romanesque façade.

The church is just as chastely beautiful inside (Eufemia was, after all, a maiden martyr), and today usually houses an exhibition appealing to the visitor on behalf of the under-privileged and suffering of this world – again appropriate, for Eufemia herself was savagely tortured before being thrown to wild beasts. If you have time to sit down here it is worth trying to understand how the Romanesque builders achieved their effect, for although the decoration is sparse, spatially the church is complex. And this is the only church in Umbria to have been built with a women's gallery.

Now return to the cathedral square. A feeling of peace always surges over me as I walk down the Via dell'Arringo and approach the Duomo of Spoleto, especially in the evening when it is floodlit. A fourteenth-century portico fronts the cool twelfth-century west façade, whose building was made necessary by Barbarossa's vicious destruction of the previous cathedral in 1155. Although the pattern is recogniz-ably Umbrian, piercing the façade are no fewer than seven rose windows. Four light the first tier, which until 1198 represented the height of this cathedral apart from a tympanun. As in Santa Eufemia, the austerity of the decora-tion enormously enhances its effect. An unfussy cornice runs along the top of this tier, and the central rose has a frame held up by columns and caryatids, with the symbols of the four evangelists at each corner.

In 1198 it was decided to add another tier to the cathedral. It was never totally finished, for three spaces, in the shape of shallow pointed arches, were left for decoration with mosaics. Only the central one has been filled. Thank heavens no lesser artist has since tried to match this work, depicting Christ blessing us, seated between the Virgin Mary and St John. The otherwise unknown genius who created it was proud enough to sign the mosaic with his name, Solsterno, and the date, 1207.

Apart from its jaunty pointed cap, the campanile is even sterner than the Romanesque façade. The portico by Ambrogio Barocci of Milan and Pippo di Antonio of

Florence, though built nearly 200 years after the rest was finished, has a Renaissance dignity that matches everything perfectly. As a result, when you go inside the Duomo and find that you are in a mid-seventeenth-century Florentine building an initial sense of disappointment is inevitable.

The antidote is to look around for some of the exceedingly fine works of art housed here. Pope Urban III commissioned the reconstruction of the interior, and his bust – by no less a genius than Bernini – is seen on the inside wall of the façade. Pintoricchio frescoed the chapel of Constantino Eroli. Annibale Caracci painted a 'Madonna and Child' with saints on the right wall of the south transept. And in Spoleto cathedral the decoration of the apse is the last work of Botticelli's teacher, the Florentine painter Filippo Lippi. The chronicler and gossip Giorgio Vasari painted this monk as so consumed with lust that he 'would give anything to enjoy a woman he wanted'. Robert Browning took up the same theme when he portrayed Filippo Lippi musing:

> Lord, they'd have taught me Latin in pure waste!
> Flower o' the clove,
> All the Latin I construe is 'amo' I love!

None the less, for Spoleto cathedral he created a magnificent cycle depicting the Annunciation, the Nativity, the death of the Virgin Mary and her heavenly coronation. Among the group in the third scene Filippo painted himself, his son and his two assistants, Brother Diamante and Pier Matteo of Amelia. The masterpiece was created between 1467 and 1469, and in the latter year Filippo Lippi died in Spoleto. He was buried in the cathedral he had so enriched, and his son Filippino designed his tomb, which you will find in the left transept.

As you leave the cathedral the noble doorway and the elegant loggia of the sixteenth-century Palazzo Arroni entice your eyes to the south side of the piazza. The west side is bordered by the Caio Melisso theatre which Giovanni Montiroli designed in 1880 (though he was skilled enough not to destroy every aspect of the earlier theatre which stood on this spot and dated from the late seventeenth century). Walk by it along the shaded Via del Duomo which opens out on to Loreto Scelli's church of San Filippo. Although its date, 1640, is virtually the same as the reconstruction of the Duomo, its interior is luscious, and contains a bizarre sight. In a glass coffin to one side of the altar lies the waxen corpse of the Blessed Don Pietro Bonelli, who died in 1935. He died in poverty, having founded a Society of the Holy Family to take in orphans, the blind and deaf-mutes. Don Pietro sleeps humbly, awaiting canonization.

More steps opposite the church lead down to Via Minervio. If you took the first right from here you would reach the pretty church of San Giovanni e Paolo, consecrated in 1174, but you would probably have to remain content with admiring its exterior, since it has been deconsecrated and is almost always closed. You might be lucky to arrive here between 10.00 and noon (or 11.00 on feast days), in which case do rush to get inside, for here are two specially interesting frescos: one of the earliest portraits of St Francis of Assisi, and another depicting the martyrdom of St Thomas à Becket.

If, as mostly happens with me, you arrive at the wrong time, continue instead to the end of Via Minervio, turn right, take the first left and cross the road to walk down a narrow arched street into the wide Piazza Edmondo de Amicis. Fronting this piazza is the lovely arched doorway of the church of San Nicolò di Bari, founded in 1304 and dedicated to the man whose image eventually developed into that of our own Father Christmas. Next to it is the restored cloister (open except on Tuesdays from 10.00 to 13.00 and from 15.00 to 18.00) which belonged to a monastery that was once a powerhouse of Spoletan Renaissance humanism. Even Martin Luther stayed here, in 1512, the year he became a Doctor of Divinity and sub-prior of his own convent at Wittenberg. Deconsecrated in the nineteenth century, this historic building became first an ironworks and then a covered market selling truffles and cloth.

105

Take the Via Gregorio Elladio north from the church
façade past the wall of the cloister. You reach a thirteenth-
century tower, the Torre dell'Olio, with a piazza named after
it. Thirty paces down, the steep Via di Porta Fuga leads under
the powerful twelfth-century Porta Fuga past the ancient
city walls. Today the old tower is sandwiched between later
buildings but still vigorously stubs itself into the sky above
them. Porta Fuga means 'gate of flight', and a Latin inscription on it explains why its other name is Hannibal's gate, for
after Hannibal had destroyed the troops of Flaminius near
Lake Trasimeno he marched on Spoleto, only to be promptly
repulsed.

Climb back to Via Gregorio Elladio and turn right along
Via Pierleone to come to the pink and white church of San
Domenico, begun in the thirteenth century and finished 200
years later. Vast and cool, it retains exquisite frescos, the
most moving undoubtedly that on the left-hand wall depicting the Virgin Mary holding the corpse of her dead son. Over
the high altar hangs another religious masterpiece, a
fourteenth-century crucifixion painted on wood, the blood
spurting obscenely from Jesus's side.

Almost immediately after the church stands the lavish
Palazzo Collicola, built by Sebastiano Cipriani in 1737. By
climbing the steps opposite this palazzo and walking up Via
Plinio il Giovane you come upon the deconsecrated church
of San Lorenzo, a touching twelfth-century former house of
God whose two little bells no longer call anyone to worship. I
have been told that there are fine thirteenth- and fourteenth-
century frescos inside, but have never managed to gain
admittance to see them.

Turn right here up Via delle Terme, looking out for Via
Sant'Agata, where buttresses support the thirteenth- and
fourteenth-century Palazzo Corvi, which in truth looks more
like a fortress than a palace. Sometimes I wonder whether
Spoleto is in danger of totally secularizing itself, for next to
this palazzo is the Romanesque arcade of yet another deconsecrated church, Sant'Agata, an arcade held up by two stone

pillars with simple carved foliage for capitals. Precious work of art that it is, Sant'Agata is less forlorn than San Lorenzo, since today it serves as the offices of those charged with restoring Spoleto's historic architecture.

At the top of this street you reach the Piazza della Libertà, to find what I think is the most enchanting Roman theatre in Umbria. Walk down the steps at the corner of the seventeenth-century Palazzo Ancaiani and you can explore this theatre at will, wandering through its arcades, climbing its stepped seats, imagining the classical actors performing where now the apse of the church of St Agata juts out on to the stage. The gates of the theatre are unlocked daily between 09.00 and 13.00 and between 15.00 and 19.00.

At the diagonally opposite corner of the piazza you find Via Brignone. A plaque on the corner house proclaims that this was the home of Francesco Possenti. Born in 1838, the eleventh child of a lawyer (there were eventually thirteen children in all), this extraordinary young man was educated by the Spoletan Jesuits. He vowed that he would join the Jesuits if God cured him of consumption. God did, but Francesco became a member of the Passionist order instead. He took the name Gabriele dell'Addolorata (Gabriel of Our Lady of Sorrows). Continually doing penances and mortifying himself, he died of tuberculosis at the age of twenty-four. Unlike Blessed Don Pietro Bonelli who is still waiting, Francesco is now St Gabriel of Our Lady of Sorrow; but even he had to wait until 1920 for canonization, so the time of his admirable fellow-Christian in the church of San Domenico may eventually come.

Walking up Via Brignone you pass the seventeenth-century Palazzo Mauri and then see ahead the Arco di Monterone, a Roman gate which has stood here since the third century BC. Turn left to walk along Via dell'Arco di Druso, to discover a yet more impressive Roman arch, this one built over two centuries later by the senate of Spoleto in honour of the son of Tiberius after his death in AD 23. The eighteenth-century church of Sant'Isacco next to it boasts a pretty cloister and rises over a twelfth-century crypt which abuts on to a former Roman temple.

These steep streets call for pauses, and in Spoleto a lively spot for pausing is the Piazza del Mercato, which you reach from here by continuing past the seventeenth-century Palazzo Leti and taking your place in the sun at a table outside one of the cafés in the square. Piazza Mercato lives up to its name by hosting a fruit and vegetable market every morning. Here you can buy roast pork from stall-holders who cut slices from a whole pig and succulently stuff them between saltless bread. Pigeons wash themselves in the piazza fountain, which looks as if it springs from the front of a church. In fact the gushing water was added in 1746 to an earlier monument which was erected in honour of Pope Urban VII.

A sign points from the corner of this piazza up to the Casa Romana, a Roman house built in the first century AD; in a few moments you reach a flight of steps where there ought to be another sign in order to find this house. What you discover there is a notice pointing up the steps to the city art gallery (the Pinoteca Communale). At the top of the steps rises a curious flame-like bronze statue, quite successful in its abstract fashion.

On the left of this piazza stands the Palazzo Communale, built in the thirteenth, seventeenth and eighteenth centuries, incorporating both the art gallery and the municipal hall. In case you cannot tell the time by the sundial on the wall, a clock above it offers an alternative method and another one also tells you the day of the month. Then you discover that quite by chance you were right to come here to get into the Roman house. Ring on the door of the municipal hall and the custodian of the Roman house will let you into the ancient home on payment of a mere 1,000 lire.

It opens from 09.00 to 12.00 and from 15.00 to 18.00 every day except Tuesday, as does the city art gallery to which entry is free. The treasures are many. I greatly recommend a pause in room II, which is devoted to the painter Giovanni di

Pietro, who lived from the mid-fifteenth century till 1528 and is known as Spagna.

The Roman remains of Spoleto are truly remarkable, matching and (because some of them are still intact) in some ways superior to those evocative ones we have seen at Carsulae. Apart from the remains we have already observed – the theatre, the gate built in the third century BC, the Roman arch built in honour of Drusus in AD 23, a Roman temple and a Roman house – Spoleto has also preserved a little Roman bridge thrown across the river a century before the birth of Jesus. The medieval city walls rise from pre-Christian foundations, whose stones you can still trace. Consider too what you cannot see. Spoleto cathedral rises over the site of a church built by the Romans. The Piazza del Mercato stands on the site of the old Roman forum and the Rocca itself on the foundations of a Roman acropolis. Spoleto also possesses an amphitheatre, but few get to see it since the city has chosen to make it the site of the army barracks.

On this Roman base grew up a higgledy-piggledy medieval city, its intricate charm enhanced by its curious hillside site. Vicolo della Basilica, the street at the far corner of the Piazza del Commune after you have re-entered it by the flight of steps leading up from the Roman house, takes you off to the right into a maze of irregular medieval alleyways, shady on the hottest of days. If you have not a moment or two to explore them, simply walk on into Piazza Bernardino Campello. On the right is a fine seventeenth-century palazzo. Ahead is the crumbling, once superb, Romanesque church of San Simone e Giuda. Water gushes from a wall through the mouth of a grotesque face, a fountain set here in the mid-seventeenth century. Part of this piazza has been pleasingly turned into a little tree-shaded park, with children's slides, and seats for their parents or grandparents. Above, on the left, towers Matteo Gattapone's Rocca.

Of the five major Umbrian hill-towns, Spoleto has been unjustly neglected. Annually from mid-June to mid-July it sponsors the 'Festival of Two Worlds', attracting renowned musicians, opera and ballet companies (its information office is at no. 9 Piazza del Duomo, tel. 0743 40396).

Spoleto is not short of tourist shops, with antique specialists clustering around the Piazza del Mercato. But no pressing need to cater for tourism has swallowed up the city's old ways. Its most fashionable shopping street, Corso Garibaldi, attractively mingles *haute couture* and leather goods with more homely fish shops. The latter open out on to the streets, as they have done here for centuries. Swordfish lie sliced up on slabs. Nearby, garden shops stand side by side with galleries selling cut glass. Giacomo Leopardi lived at no. 19, so an inscription tells you, between 12 November 1822 and 4 September 1830.

You can eat cheaply and satisfyingly by choosing a tourist menu, or stunningly by searching out the gastronomic specialities of the city. Look out for *palomba in salmi* (wood pigeons cooked in a pungent sauce of truffles, capers, ham and anchovies). When it rains the Spoletans, instead of complaining, rejoice that succulent little snails will shortly be found on the hillsides outside their city. As they collect them they also pick a species of thyme named *serpullo*. They throw the snails and the *serpullo* into a pot with a handful of fennel and serve them as *lumachine al serpullo*.

Just as delightful is to gather together a picnic basket of local wine, cheese, bread and fruit, before driving out through the thirteenth-century Monterone gate and winding your way for eight kilometres up to Monteluco. On the way you pass the church of San Pietro, whose twelfth-century façade is carved with men fighting lions, Jesus walking on the water and human legs dangling helplessly from a devil's cooking pot. Another soul is found wanting in the balance and is abandoned by the Archangel to the devil. The seventeenth-century interior is richly decked with crimson damask embroidered with gold braid down all its pillars and over its pulpit, and a golden *baldacchino* is suspended over the high altar.

The road now curves up to Monteluco, offering heavenly

views of Spoleto as it rises. On the way you pass the twelfth-century church of San Giuliano, whose porch incorporates fragments of the sixth-century church it replaced. Monteluco itself lies 830 metres above sea-level and is worth visiting for its panorama alone. St Francis founded a convent here and you can visit the sanctuary between 08.00 and 13.00 and between 16.00 and 20.00. Here there are hotels and a bar which in no way disturb the peace of the leafy spot, as well as countless little tables and benches where you can enjoy your picnic under the trees.

From Spoleto let me propose two round trips in order properly to savour this dream country. The first takes in some of the most awe-inspiring and least-known landscapes of Umbria and also reaches ancient cities rich in intensely passionate Christian history. The second, as well as visiting smiling villages and secluded sanctuaries, includes an unexpected touch of the macabre. The first trip is a long one, but two of its sites are of such importance that if you cannot find time to pursue the route at leisure, simply drive to Norcia and Cascia and back. The second trip is an easier drive, calculated to entrance lovers of ancient romantic monasteries and make the flesh of children creep.

Spoleto is the gateway to the eastern part of the region of Umbria. Leave the city by the Porta Garibaldi and watch for the signs for the E395, which snakes up through mountains with deep ravines falling away first to the left and then to the right. The road peaks and then descends, offering views of the forested, majestic Sibilline mountains, which here are high enough to lose themselves in the clouds. On a sudden bend Vallo di Nera appears over to the right, its white houses rising away from the road like a creamy wedding-cake set on a green table. Like most children's treats, in my experience, it happens to be just out of reach, so we must explore it on our way back from Cascia and now drive north-east instead.

The route descends through the little hillside village of Piedipaterno, which is still a mountain settlement situated 333 metres above sea-level. At Piedipaterno there is a

Romanesque church dedicated to the Santissima Annunzi-
ate dell'Eremita, save that here they call it the Romitorio.
From this village take route 209 north-east. It becomes even
more scenic, with the mountains rising precipitately on
either side, an occasional weary widow toiling up from one
village to the next. The scenery is among the most sensational
in Umbria – outcrops of pink rocks tracing their fantastic
patterns, modulating into grey, white and black, though
these colours never overwhelm the predominant glowing
pink.

Over to the left you glimpse the hamlet of Cerreto di
Spoleto, rising 560 metres above sea-level. Then ahead, on
their own eminence, rise the old towers and bastions of Borgo
Cerreto, strategically situated above the confluence of the
Rivers Vigi and Nera. For its thirteenth-century church of
San Lorenzo a friar named Francesco da Pescia painted in
1551 a splendid 'Madonna of the Choristers', and an unknown
architect designed its ravishing façade and rose window.

If you adore superb monastic churches, two and a half
kilometres after Borgo Cerreto look for the signs pointing left,
for a brief diversion to the north (no more than three
kilometres) leading to the excellently restored monastic
buildings of San Giacomo close to Cerreto di Spoleto. The
buildings date from the thirteenth to the sixteenth centuries
and their frescos glow with the mysticism of the fourteenth
century. Cerreto di Spoleto itself, lying at the foot of the
1,428-metre-high Mount Maggiore, competes with this
gem with two more lovely churches, the church of the
Annunciata and the church of Santa Maria de Libera, both
crammed with priceless religious art.

Return to the 209 and drive on to defensively walled
Triponzo. An ancient tower still looks as if it might struggle to
repel invaders. Triponzo means 'three bridges', necessary to
negotiate the confluence of the Nera and the Corno; and the
town's site made it vital in the Middle Ages to protect itself
from attack. What Triponzo was not prepared for was an
earth tremor of 1974, which led some of its citizens to leave

and find homes elsewhere. The parish church is worth turning off the road to see, to enjoy its mid-sixteenth-century
doorway and a curious wooden font carved at the same time.

From here there are two ways to Norcia, depending on how
much time you have. The swiftest way turns right along the
SS320 to burrow through Mount Cavogna. Tunnels enable
you to avoid clambering around its 1,417-metre-high peak.
(Italian law requires motorists to switch on their headlights
if a tunnel is not lit.) The route becomes all the more exciting
because notices continually warn drivers of falling rocks,
though in the most dangerous spots the authorities have
thoughtfully worked out ways of catching these before they
smash through the roof of your car.

At Serravalle, close to which is the quaint campanile of the
thirteenth-century church of San Claudio, instead of following the SS320 due south, continue east along the 396. The
valley is opening out and Norcia is at hand, situated in an
amphitheatre of mountains whose peaks are too high to be
wooded. On the great gate of the city you read the inscription
VETVSTA NURSIA and drive on to the central piazza.

The longer route to Norcia takes in some of Umbria's most
entrancing villages and ravishing scenery. From Triponzo
follow the 209 north-east, passing through San Lázzaro,
whose waterfall cascades down a rocky thirty metres, to the
spot where the region of the Marches puts a little finger into
Umbria. This is winter sports country, and the snows linger
on the mountainsides. In ancient villages dotting the slopes
and sheltered in valleys, old men snooze on chairs in the
streets, while their sons and daughters grow black olives,
collect truffles and milk sheep. One of these villages,
Castelvecchio, is said to produce the finest lamb in Italy. On
great occasions even the old men wake up to join in the
region's traditional festivals – the Feast of the Assumption at
Ferragosto and those that honour local saints (St Rita's Day,
on 22 May at San Lázzaro; St Bartholomew's Day, on 22
August at Todiano; the Feast of Santa Maria della Pietà, on 7
June at Preci; the Feast of the Madonna del Soccorso, on the

second Sunday in August at Castelvecchio).

The 209 now turns west to reach Preci. Preci's castle dates back to the thirteenth century, though it was several times damaged by earthquakes, as well as being sacked by the Norcians in 1527, so the present structure is no more than 450 years old. The Palazzo Communale retains its fourteenth-century elegance. The church of Santa Maria incorporates a Romanesque porch in its Gothic façade. Its font was made in 1521, and the church also treasures a chilling fifteenth-century *pietà*.

This medieval village seems so remote from the rest of the world that I remain astonished at learning of the fame of its surgeons in the sixteenth and seventeenth centuries, especially its eye-surgeons. One of them operated on the cataracts of Queen Elizabeth I of England; in 1620 another became doctor to Sultan Mohammed; and a third operated on the cataracts of the Empress Eleonora Gonzaga.

Drive south-east through Piedivalle, whose sixteenth-century parish church is rich in contemporary frescos. Just outside Piedivalle rises the ancient convent of San Eutizio, a miraculously preserved Benedictine convent, with a Romanesque church built around 1190 by an architect known as Maestro Pietro, and blessed with fourteenth-century cloisters. The region is rich in isolated, exquisite villages, such as Todiano, some fifteen kilometres south (you have to turn left off the 209 to reach it), where the parish church unexpectedly contains a painting by Filippo Lippi and the castello dates back to the thirteenth century.

Drive back to the 209 which then winds through Campi, with the delightful medieval village of Campi Vecchio rising above it, and then curves for a mere twelve kilometres to reach Norcia.

Norcia is famous for two things: pork and St Benedict. In the past, the Norcians say (and who is to doubt them), this region produced the finest surgeons in the world because for centuries they had been practising by carving up pigs. Even today Norcians each year venture into the rest of Italy to

114

carve pigs for farmers who lack their skill. Their peculiar talent has added two words to the Italian language: *norcineria*, which the Tuscans and the Romans now use for a charcuterie, especially one specializing in pork, and *norcino*, which means pork butcher.

Throughout Umbria roadside vans sell *porchetta*. On their counter lies a whole roasted pig that has been deliciously stuffed, its flesh spiced with garlic. Beginning at the rump, the mobile butchers carve slices for their customers. Sometimes served with a huge chunk of bread, sometimes simply wrapped in paper, one slice along with a glass of red wine (preferably a strong one, say a Montefalco DOC) is, for me, enough for a complete midday meal.

Porchetta is a delicacy invented by the Norcians. Norcian ham is similarly spicy, lacking the fattiness of the *prosciutto* which you find in other regions. The local pigs are small. The little victims guzzle acorns and chestnuts, heedless of their doom.

The tables of the trattorie of Norcia, often serving this spicy ham with mushrooms and truffles, bear witness to the age-long tradition of Norcian butchers and pig-farmers. If you ask any Umbrian what are the prized dishes of the region, the answer will be *salame norcino* or *conchiglia alla norcina*, a local shellfish dish.

Norcia enjoys three annual festivals. One celebrates its folklore, with floats parading the streets. A second, in June, gives thanks for the flowers that festoon the Sibilline mountains. The third, held in autumn, honours the Umbrian truffle.

In the centre of the main square of Norcia (Piazza San Benedetto) a statue of St Benedict, sculpted by Giuseppe Prinzi in 1880, bears witness to the city's greatest son. It carries an inscription stating that in 1958 Pope Pius XII declared St Benedict to be the 'Padre dell'Europa Christiana'.

Why should a man born in Norcia in the year 480 be judged the father of European Christianity? Benedict's family was

115

rich enough to send him to study in Rome, where the papacy was supporting a number of Byzantine centres of monastic life. These inspired Benedict to take the monastic habit himself, especially as the debauched life of Rome revolted him. With two disciples he settled near Subiaco, not however living as part of the community but building themselves hermitages, each finding his own grotto in which to devote himself entirely to prayer and the spiritual life without the company or distraction even of like-minded Christians.

Although Benedict could miraculously cure the sick, and once miraculously enabled a disciple to run across a lake, a local lord became his enemy, and this prompted him to think of developing his way of life in a new fashion and in a new place. He dreamt of founding a great monastic community which might reform and inspire all Western Christians while still allowing men to live virtually separate lives. At Montecassino, half-way between Rome and Naples, he found a fortified hill which the pagans had long regarded as sacred. Benedict and his followers moved there, destroyed the holy places of the poor pagans and set up a series of oratories in their stead.

So great was his influence that others founded similar Italian monasteries. His twin sister Scholastica came to Montecassino and there founded a sister community of nuns. Since Benedict's rule meant that he and Scholastica were barred from each other's convents, they met once a year in a house outside Montecassino. On the day Scholastica knew she was dying she asked her brother to stay with her over-night. He refused, but Scholastica prayed that he might be prevented from leaving her. God granted her request, charitably overruling Benedict's own stern rule. After Scholastica's death her brother placed her body in his own tomb, giving instructions that when he died his own corpse should be placed beside hers. So, as Pope Gregory the Great put it, 'The bodies of these two, whose minds were always united in Jesus, were not separated in death.'

What made Benedict renowned was the rule he left for his

monastic communities. At that time the Goths were hammering at the bulwarks of society. Just as Western civilization seemed to be disintegrating, especially in Gaul and Italy, here was a firm basis for little cells of Christian order and stability that could survive the northern invasions as well as the splitting up of the Roman empire. Was Benedict aware that this was to be his legacy to the West? Probably not; but as you read his rule, scarcely 12,000 words in all, much of it drawn from the Bible, you spot its essential practicality. 'As much as possible, the monastery should be constructed so that everything needful, such as water, a mill, provision for household crafts, should be found within it,' he wrote. His aim was not simply pragmatism. This instruction was designed to prevent monks from leaving the precincts of the monastery and thus submitting themselves to the temptations of the outside world. But as Don David Knowles has written, 'Here, as with so much in the rule, the spiritual advantage carried with it others of a material and social kind.' Professor Knowles added, 'All other forms of higher organization might dissolve, whether in empire, province or diocese, but this family would survive.'

Of course the rule of St Benedict is also filled with spiritual advice. One and a half millennia later what strikes me as so acute about these spiritual maxims is that they are as laconically practical as his instructions for building a monastery. If you feel you ought to pray, St Benedict orders, don't brood hesitantly outside the chapel. 'Go straight in and pray.' Small wonder that forty-five years or so after Benedict's death, Pope Gregory the Great felt inspired to write a life of this obscure Umbrian. St Gregory's life of Benedict remained a classic throughout the Middle Ages. As the Pope observed of the Umbrian saint, 'He wrote a rule for monks which is remarkable for its lucidity and order.' And, as we have seen, his Benedictine followers gave generously of their lands and churches to St Francis. One should go further and ask whether, without the achievement of St Benedict of Norcia to build on, Francis would have accomplished what he did?

It is, for instance, the rule of St Benedict that insists on the absolute renunciation of personal property for anyone who wishes to follow the religious life, a rule later taken up with such gusto by the Franciscans. From the day of a monk's profession, Benedict insisted, 'He will not even own his own body.'

St Benedict laid down much more: a severe regime of daily prayer and praise; a monastic structure with an abbot whose rule was supreme; and many hours devoted to study and learning. As I stand in the square at Norcia, only my foolish twentieth-century notion (derived from living in our over-large cities) that this was some backwater in the sixth century AD makes it difficult to believe that such a creative source of a new form of Western culture was nurtured here.

Yet Norcia had undergone a long and sometimes trau-matic history well before the birth of its most famous son. A Sabine city conquered by the Romans 290 years before the birth of Jesus, it retains many remains of this era, though most of them are today incorporated in its later buildings. Norcia sided with Scipio in the Second Punic War. It played a major role in the Roman civil wars. St Feliciano, Bishop of Foligno, had converted Norcia to Christianity 250 years before St Benedict was born.

After Benedict's death Norcia suffered grievously at the hands of the invading heathen, was sacked by the Goths, invaded by the Lombards and Saracens, and torn between Guelph and Ghibelline. The town became prosperous again in the Middle Ages, a commune and the seat of a papal prefecture. In consequence most of its great buildings date from around the fourteenth century.

The attractive church of San Benedetto in Piazza San Benedetto is in fact older in origin than its present form, which dates from 1389. The economy of the design of the Gothic façade lends power to the single rose window, guarded by the symbols of the four evangelists. Two niches flank the carved doorway, one with a statue of St Benedict, the other with a statue of his twin sister. In the lunette of the doorway is a colourful depiction of the Madonna and two angels. Tradition has it that San Benedetto is built over the house where the two saints were born, and if you go into the crypt you can certainly see through a grille the foundations of a Roman house. For good luck pious Italians throw coins through the grille. What seems more likely is that we are on the site of a pre-Christian sanctuary, for here too are remains of a Roman building dating from the first century AD.

This church, like much else in Norcia, suffered not only from the assaults of the heathen but also from numerous earthquakes. Surprisingly, it has managed to retain a late sixth-century oratory. Before leaving the church, look for a fourteenth-century fresco depicting Benedict and Scholastica on either side of Jesus, and the mystical sixteenth-century fresco depicting the 'Madonna of Mercy'.

As you walk out of San Benedetto into the sunlight, the steps of the Palazzo Communale rise to your right. Its fourteenth-century façade with a thirteenth-century porch was subsequently much embellished, but the seventeenth-century belfry is a fair match of the fourteenth-century campanile of San Benedetto. The loggia was not added till 1876 and is by Domenico Mollaioli. The nearby church of Santa Maria Misericordia is a similar blend of styles – polite and simple outside, elaborately classical inside.

At the opposite side of the piazza from the Palazzo Communale is the Castellina. Pope Julius III ordered its construction (on the site of a pagan temple dedicated to the goddess Fortuna) in 1554, and the architect was Jacopo Barozzi da Vignola. From the outside the Castellina is stern, a fortress with four corner bastions, but inside Vignola created an exquisite courtyard. Today the Castellina is the home of the Norcian city museum and shelters some lovely medieval statues in wood and stone and terracotta.

At the south corner of the piazza stands the Duomo, Santa Maria Argentea, with its haughty belfry. Built in 1560, rebuilt after the earthquakes of 1703 and 1730, the cathedral was extensively restored in the mid-nineteenth century. It takes its name from a former medieval church, remains of which you can spot in the ogival doorway on the left side.

The city holds much else of charm: the church of Sant' Agostino, built in the fourteenth century but now endowed with a seventeenth-century interior; the eighteenth-century church of San Filippo; and the unusual Tempietto, a mid-fourteenth-century building by Vanni Tuzi who set semi-circular arcades on two sides of his little square building. The arcades are neatly decorated with reliefs of animals, foliage and symbols of the passion. Twelve kilometres outside the city (leave Norcia by the Porta Ascolana and take the road for Antrodoco) is the Madonna delle Neve, a Renaissance church dating from the second half of the sixteenth century. Octagonal outside, with a Greek cross inside, its frescos, dating from the same century, are by Camillo and Fabio Angelucci.

Don't depart from Norcia without exploring its shops as well as its restaurants. You can buy beautiful hand-made woollen garments here, as well as locally spun yarns from shops advertising *arte della lana*; and I can rarely escape without buying a piece of the ravishing hand-made lace of the city, *merletto fatto a mano*.

Norcian restaurants, as well as serving succulent pork, also profit by being not far from the easternmost hill town in the whole of Umbria, Castelluccio, for this town produces the finest lentils in the whole of Italy. You reach this stunning spot, alas, by the most tortuous diversion, a thirty-kilometre journey through the mountains and one which I recommend only if you are planning to return and spend the night in one of Norcia's hotels. To reach Castelluccio drive south from the city, watching for the turn-off left.

Castelluccio nestles like a white bowler hat on its round hill, 1,452 metres above sea-level. As you approach it, the route crosses a remarkable plain, created from a dried-up lake some eighteen kilometres long. Every May when the buttercups and narcissi are blooming on the plain of Castelluccio, its citizens disport themselves in their festival of the blossoms. Hang-gliders set off from here on their perilous flight. Sheep are reared here, and in consequence mozzarella cheese and lamb from Castelluccio make their proud appearance in the restaurants of Norcia. Some say that the lamb is as succulent as that from Castelvecchio.

From Norcia an eighteen-kilometre drive takes you west along the 396 to Serravalle and from there south, winding down the 320 along the valley of the River Corno to Cascia. Cascia has suffered tasteless expansion, boasting swimming pools, tennis courts and nondescript hotels. But its zigzag walls and its site on a hilltop ensure that, in the end, the heart of Cascia can never be spoilt. High above the town as you negotiate the hair-raising drive rises the ruined fifteenth-century Rocca and the medieval church of Sant'Agostino. But the kernel of Cascia today is the sanctuary of St Rita, with a colonnaded arcade leading to it, and notices warning you to remain prayerfully silent.

A twentieth-century sanctuary to a fifteenth-century saint is a phenomenon that needs some explanation. Rita was born in 1381 in the central Apennines to elderly parents, who thwarted her desire to take up the religious life by insisting that she take a husband. Dutifully she did. Arranged marriages often thrive better than those entered under the wayward impulse of romantic love, but this one was disastrous. Rita's husband was cruel and dissolute. She bore him two sons, who proved equally as aggressive as their father. After eighteen years of silent misery, she was widowed, her husband's corpse brought home covered with fatal wounds after a quarrel that had turned to violence.

His sons vowed vengeance. Now Rita displayed the chilling tenacity of an authentic medieval saint. Rather than allow her own offspring to risk eternal damnation by murdering those who had killed her husband, she prayed that they might die; and so they did.

At last, freed from the cares of the world, Rita begged admission to the nunnery of Cascia. She was rejected, on the grounds that only virgins were fit for religious life. She refused to be put down, repeatedly persisting in asking the nuns to take her in. Her determination was rewarded, for the rules were relaxed and Rita became a nun. Her superiors, though, perhaps annoyed at her persistence, continually attempted to try the saint's patience. Once the abbess ordered Rita to water an obviously dead plant. Rita humbly continued to tend the rotting piece of wood.

She was rewarded in a fashion that recalls St Francis's stigmata. One day as she prayed before a crucifix a thorn broke loose from the cruel crown around her Saviour's head and lodged itself in her temple. The wound soon stank so much that only when Rita prayed for temporary remission (for instance when she felt the need to make a pilgrimage elsewhere) did the suppuration momentarily disappear. She was now obliged to live alone, to spare her fellow-sisters the deathly odour that exuded from her.

Rita's frail body began to waste away. As she lay dying an old friend brought her a rose from the Apennines, and this has now become St Rita's symbol. She died on 22 May 1477. Then nature reversed itself. The frail corpse refused to fall into dust. As you can see in the glass coffin at Cascia where it is today displayed, the earthly body of St Rita has remained incorrupt.

Rita was not beatified until 1626. She was canonized only in 1900 – hence her unexpectedly pseudo-Byzantine but essentially art deco shrine at Cascia. Over the door is inscribed a cryptic legend, taken from the saint's former sarcophagus, which would be unintelligible to anyone unfamiliar with the life of Rita:

SALVE RITA VAS AMORIS SPOSA DOLOROSA
TV DE SPINIS SALVATORIS PVLCHRA NASCERIS UT ROSA

(Hail Rita, prophetess of love and sorrowful wife;
From the thorns of the Saviour you were born as a beautiful rose.)

The Augustinian nuns of Cascia keep alive her memory, and no one can miss her superb sanctuary, built between 1937 and 1947, with its vividly coloured frescos painted by various twentieth-century hands. It would be a pity for the visitor not to explore the rest of Cascia. The church of Sant'Agostino, which we have already spotted and which Rita loved, was built in 1380 and boasts an orderly Gothic porch. Santa Maria, where Rita was baptized, was built in 1300, and close by is a fountain guarded by a Romanesque stone lion. The façade of the church of San Francesco dates from 1424 and is pierced by another Gothic doorway and a delicate rose window. The fifteenth-century church of Sant'Antonio is splendidly frescoed, with two mid-fifteenth-century paintings (of Jesus carrying his cross and then being nailed to it) by Nicola da Siena. In the same church the pink horse of a Roman soldier in Nicola's depiction of Calvary reminds one of the daring artistic liberties taken in the same century by the Florentine genius Paolo Uccello. As for secular buildings, the Palazzo Communale of Cascia abuts on to a ponderous old bell-tower.

Twelve kilometres south-west of Cascia is Monteleone di Spoleto. The Tore dell'Orologio, the ancient towered doorway of its former castle, no longer defends the city but welcomes you. The fourteenth-century Palazzo Bernabò is both haughty and good-mannered. And two lions placidly rest on the corbel of the Gothic porch of the church of San Francesco.

Now wind north for Poggiodomo, shaded from the southwest by Mount Carpenale and graced with a church dedicated to San Pietro which is decorated with fourteenth- and fifteenth-century frescos. As you drive on, the road forks left to reach Vallo di Nera, which exemplifies the extraordinary artistic riches of this region of Italy. The church of Santa Maria points to the antiquity of the village, for it dates from the twelfth century and is embellished with an ogival arched doorway over which is a rose window. Inside it you will discover a moving Romanesque crucifix. Further up in the village is the parish church of San Giovanni Battista, this one built 100 years later, sporting another rose window, its apse frescoed in 1536 by Jacopo Siculo. The tabernacle dates from 1504, and in the ambulatory is a thirteenth-century painting of the 'Madonna and Child'. In admiring such treasures we are of course simply exploring a small, relatively obscure Umbrian village. From Vallo di Nera rejoin the 395 just beyond Piedipaterno and twist your way sinuously back to Spoleto.

My second round trip from Spoleto leaves the city by the road for Foligno and Assisi and again snakes off to the right in the direction of Norcia and Cascia by way of the 395. Just beyond Piedipaterno it forks sharply right to run south-west along the 209 and the valley of the River Nera. Medieval villages perch on rocky hills: Castel San Felice, whose church of San Felice has a splendid twelfth-century façade; and magical Sant'Anatolia di Narco, walled since the fourteenth century, still preserving remnants of its medieval castle and proud of its two fine churches, one built in the thirteenth century, the other in the 1570s.

The village of Scheggino next falls down the hillside, walled since the twelfth century, sanctified by the thirteenth-century church of San Nicolò (its interior remodelled in the fifteenth century and beautifully frescoed) and protected by a forlorn tower. Just over four kilometres further on appears the hamlet of San Valentino whose inhabitants worship in their twelfth-century church.

Keep an eye open for the sign at Sambucheto which points right, by way of an extremely sharp bend, towards the Abbazia di San Pietro in Valle. If you have simply glanced at the villages so far, spare more time for this ruined abbey, which was built between the sixth and eighth centuries. The side road climbs up into the hills through a minuscule village where, in the middle, likely as not the women will be scrubbing clothes at the public washing place. The Nera valley now appears to your left in all its grandeur. On the other flank is an abandoned, fortified village. Then the terrific abbey of San Pietro comes into view. Park under the olives and if you need some refreshment walk across to the restaurant where you can eat in the open air.

Across the valley the cliffs are now almost sheer. Your first impression of the surprising size of the abbey is gained from walking past its high walls, as far as the five-storeyed Romanesque campanile, square and simply decorated. The outer courtyard of the abbey has a well, and over the door as you enter is a faded fresco of the Crucified, with two saints. Walk through to the yellow-plastered cloister, where round arches spring from stone pillars, and more slender pillars hold up the balustrade. Opposite this balustrade steps lead into the church. Two sternly comical figures carved in the tenth century guard its entrance. St Paul brandishes his sword and St Peter seems ready to bash an unwelcome intruder over the head with his cross. The person who carved them must have had specific models in mind, for the faces of the two saints are quite distinct. Immediately inside the abbey you come across a magical frieze, in which St Sebastian is, in my view, painted with the hair and face of a very pretty girl.

The roof of this abbey has been missing for a long time, and it seems remarkable that the rest of the building has stood up so well to the ravages of the weather. Once the whole church was frescoed and you can still dimly make out scenes from the Old and New Testaments; but now the only really clear paintings are found in the apse. The furnishings of this apse are remarkable, including a Lombardic altar signed by the man who carved it (VRSVS MAGESTER FECIT). The abbey of San Pietro houses altogether five Roman sarcophagi, three built into the structure, the finest (I think) that which holds up the pillar to the right of the apse.

The origin of all this splendour was the desire of two hermits named Lazarro and Giovanni to find seclusion from the cares of the sixth-century world here on the slopes of Mount Solenne.

Return from the abbey to route 209 and make your way further south-west through Macenano, where men will be playing cards outside the local bar. Shortly you are vouchsafed another glimpse of the Abbazia di San Pietro up to your right. The rocks are bare now, and some of them clearly sheer off from time to time. Ahead a twin-towered medieval castle lours from the hillside, and beneath it is Ferentillo.

Ferentillo rises on both sides of the road. Since your first aim on this round trip is to make your own flesh creep, keep looking on the left for the sign to the Museo delle Mummie, following it to park in the village square. More signs take you further, up Via Padova and round to the left up Via delle Turre as far as the fourteenth-century church of San Stefano, where the mummies of the long-dead human beings we are about to inspect have been dug up out of the chalky earth that has preserved them, to be put on display in half-open glass cases.

Here are seen French soldiers, taken prisoner and executed around 1500; one hanged, as you can clearly see, the other shot with his hands tied together. The little baby you think you spot turns out to be a bearded gnome who has kept most of his teeth. The clothing of a 300-year-old woman is virtually intact. Another dead soldier is erect not in a glass coffin but in a clock case, since his legs are so long that he stands two metres high. You peer at a sad mother and the baby she died giving birth to. The mummified bodies of two Chinese sit, unconcerned. They died at Ferentillo on their honeymoon, said the custodian. (How does he know all this?) Not long ago, he told me, someone stole the skull of one of them, but it has happily been recovered. The last mummy is that of a lawyer, killed in 1871 by robbers.

Alongside these relics, rows of skulls are set out neatly in trays, and piles of bones are tucked into the walls. I tipped the custodian 1,000 lire and fled back to the bar in the village square to wash the dust of the dead out of my throat.

The lipless grin of these mummies scarcely characterizes Ferentillo's true spirit, for the couple of medieval fortresses which dominate the village have mellowed over the centuries. At the other side of the valley is a shady park in front of another Ferentillo church, as ever with apparatus for children's games. Santa Maria was founded in the thirteenth century, much rebuilt in the sixteenth, its façade even more tampered with in our own times. Its porch dates from 1493, and it treasures a sweet fifteenth-century Madonna and two angels.

Drive on south-west down the valley, which grows wider and gentler now on its way to Terni, with hamlets sheltering on its lower slopes and others scrabbling up the rocks towards stumpy towers. Turn right twenty-four kilometres from Spoleto where you see the sign for Montefranco, which is stunningly sited on a spur, with new houses spreading out from the medieval village along the ridge.

After ten kilometres you turn right along the Via Flaminia to drive back to Spoleto. The village of Strettura rises on the right, walled and tumbledown on its hillock, and soon (as by now it is surely dusk) the road passes by the softly lit façade of San Pietro, with the illuminated Rocca of Spoleto rising ahead.

From sublimely mad Gubbio to Città di Castello

'A stone cascade upon the lower slopes of Mount Ingino' is how the art historian John White described Gubbio. He went on to acclaim this altogether astonishing Umbrian city as 'a piece of engineering on a Roman scale' and 'among the most remarkable single feats of civic planning in the history of medieval Italy'.

Notwithstanding their achievement in creating a city that is unsurpassed in the whole of Umbria, the people of Gubbio are content to consider themselves slightly batty. One of the city's most charming palaces is the thirteenth-century Palazzo del Bargello, three storeys of gracefully unpretentious Gothic architecture. Note the doors. Two of them, one huge, lead to the granaries, store-rooms and cellars. A slender, elegant one on the left opens into the living quarters above. But the most fascinating is the blocked-up 'door of the dead' (over the largest of the three still-open entrances), doors whose grim significance we have explored in Assisi.

In the square fronting the palazzo (known as the Largo del Bargello) stands a good-mannered double-bowled fountain, erected in the fifteenth century. If you run three times around this fountain, I was told, you are given a certificate as an honorary lunatic of Gubbio. 'This is how mad they are,' said my informant. Admittedly, she was not a Gubbian. What the Gubbians (who call themselves Eugubians) themselves say is that to run round it thrice makes you in every respect a citizen of their ancient commune, freed from all hypocrisy and vain show, as beguiling and unaffected as a little child. What they mean is mad, for the fountain is dedicated to lunatics and called the 'fontana die Matti'.

I did experience some of this batty unaffectedness the first time I stayed in the city. Throughout the whole night outside my hotel a clock delicately chimed both the hours and the quarters, as if to reassure us all that we hadn't overslept. I got up early, flung open the shutters to gaze over the romantic countryside from which Gubbio rises, and was waved at by two men on top of a house just below me, already laying a pantile roof in the traditional Gubbian fashion.

To start at the Largo del Bargello is to start half-way through exploring Gubbio. The powerful city overwhelms you as you drive up to its white walls; the Piazza della Signoria, flanked on the left by the mighty Palazzo dei Consoli and on the right by the Palazzo del Pretorio, already looming vastly above.

Drive in and park in Piazza Quaranta Martiri, named in honour of forty Gubbian partisans executed here by the Fascists on 19 January 1944. Here the lofty church of San Francesco gleams white, save for the brick decoration at the top of its slender octagonal campanile. The Perugian architect Fra Bevignate built it at the very end of the thirteenth century, its three aisles separated by elegant octagonal columns. This airy church has an apse decorated with mid-fifteenth-century frescos depicting scenes from the life of the Blessed Virgin Mary by a masterly Gubbian artist named Ottaviano Nelli. On a pillar to the right is an eerie representation of Jesus mocked. Disembodied hands beat him and a disembodied face spits into his face. This apse houses frescos painted over three centuries, those on the right desperately in need of sympathetic conservation and restoration. On the south wall by the altar is a deeply unsettling 'Deposition', which was painted by the Gubbian artist Virgilio Nucci in 1575.

Across the Piazza Quaranta Martiri stands the long weavers' gallery, the Loggiato dei Tiratoi dell'Arte della Lana. Here Gubbian weavers used to stretch out their dyed wool to dry. Its upper storey dates from the sixteenth century, the lower one from the late fourteenth. Since the gallery was public property, in the days when Gubbio elected Captains of the People, each one on assuming office would publicly take into his possession the loggia.

Look for a slightly weather-beaten fresco under its homely portico, representing the Virgin Mary flanked by St Peter and St Paul and painted by Bernardino di Narni in 1473. This mixture of daily work and the blessings of our unseen guardians in heaven caused no complications in any medieval mind, an observation reinforced to the left of the weavers' gallery, into which merges contentedly the church of Santa Maria dei Laici, built in 1313. If you want to go inside to see its find frescos (which include twenty-four scenes from the life of Mary, painted in the sixteenth century by the Gubbian Felice Damiano), the custodian of the key lives at no. 40.

Climb up the shaded narrow Via Piccardi. It crosses the little River Camignano, and then you turn right into Via Battilana, which after thirty metres reaches Piazza San Giovanni, a square created – so it seems – almost entirely from medieval houses. The little thirteenth-century church of San Giovanni Battista here has a much damaged Gothic porch. Its powerful campanile has been given a gentler aspect by being pierced by ogival lights. Although the interior, by comparison with San Francesco, does not house artistic treasures of mind-shattering note, do go inside if only to enjoy the bizarreness which comes from having to build a city hanging from a cliff. As you walk towards the main altar of San Giovanni Battista you suddenly realize that inside the church you are climbing uphill.

Above everything still towers the Palazzo dei Consoli. Cross the Piazza San Giovanni, and after a further twenty metres you reach Via della Repùbblica, turning left to climb still further as arched medieval streets, now bordered with trattorie, beckon enticingly on either side. At the top of the street it becomes apparent that Gubbio is doubly fortified, the Palazzo dei Consoli rising from its own powerful walls. It is worth turning left here, along Via Baldassini, to admire once again the massive genius of Matteo Gattapone to whom (however much the scholars dispute this) must surely be attributed the four enormous arches which support the Piazza della Signoria.

Walk back a little way to climb up alongside the walls of the Palazzo Pretorio by the winding steps of Via Orderigo Lucarelli. Then turn left into Piazza della Signoria. This piazza offers not only the most stupendous view across the valley to distant Umbrian hills but also a delicious treat: the sight of the chimneys and pantile roofs of the medieval city below you, a patchwork of houses huddling warmly together.

Piazza della Signoria is the annual venue on the last Sunday in May of Gubbio's crossbow *palium*. As has happened since the thirteenth century, trumpets herald the opening ceremony. Men waving and throwing into the air huge multicoloured banners signal the start of the competition. Other men in medieval costume sit before the deadliest weapon of the Middle Ages, once condemned by Pope and councils alike, but never abandoned until the invention of gunpowder in the fifteenth century. The scene is enhanced by the women of Gubbio, also bedecked in medieval costume.

A commune such as Gubbio needed its fraternity of skilled crossbowmen to protect both its high officials, as they went about their business, and also the very city itself. Gubbio's

Societas Balisteriorum was one of the most feared in central Italy, once putting to flight an army composed of men from no fewer than twelve rival cities. Today their rivals are the crossbowmen of Borgo San Sepolcro, and no doubt every single competitor aiming the ancient weapons in the Piazza della Signoria still swells with the pride of a medieval archer.

In this piazza the unfinished façade of Matteo Gattapone's Palazzo Pretorio, now Gubbio's town hall, seems dour compared with the flamboyant Palazzo dei Consoli at the opposite end of the piazza, but it possesses its own grandeur. Begun in 1349, the plan was to construct a palace twice as long as the present one. The design of the interior displays Gattapone's customary daring. He supported the three storeys of the palazzo with a single, slender octagonal column. As the column approaches each ceiling, it fans out into vaulting so mathematically spare that the very absence of decoration becomes a tasteful, even if architecturally swashbuckling, virtue.

The phrase which Professor John White applied to Gubbio, 'engineering on a Roman scale', was a deliberate reference to the fact that the Palazzo dei Consoli, though unfinished, was inaugurated on 21 April 1338, the anniversary of the founding of Rome. Gubbio set out to be a new Rome. The architect of the palazzo had begun work some decade and a half earlier. Scholars dispute who he was – either the amazing Gubbian Matteo Gattapone himself or Angelo da Orvieto. If the attribution to Angelo is correct, Orvieto rather than Rome is the real inspiration of this haughty building. I, who adore Matteo Gattapone, compromise by attributing the basic plan to Gattapone but giving Angelo the credit of designing the wonderful staircase and the Gothic doorway.

Whoever was responsible for this magnificent building, soon the consuls were installed, and an aqueduct gushed water to their new palace. As we saw, walking along Via Baldassini, Gattapone cared little for symmetry. As you stand there, gazing up at the side of the palazzo, above the huge supporting arches rises a façade whose loggia surmounts a lower row of extremely disorderly windows. Only the main façade, approached by Angelo's truly noble arched flight of steps, behaves itself in an orderly fashion. As for these steps themselves, their utilitarian aim was to allow access to the central chamber of the Palazzo dei Consoli without blocking up the rooms below.

Great architecture consists of solving apparently insuperable problems with aesthetic panache. By beginning with a shallow semicircle of steps, from which another stairway arches up to a square balcony, the master who designed the ceremonial staircase from the Piazza della Signoria up to the Palazzo dei Consoli has transformed the practical problem with which he was faced into a technically staggering work of art.

The work of art that is this whole palazzo now houses Gubbio's municipal art gallery. The earliest-known Gubbian painter whose name we know was Guido Palmerucci, who lived from the late thirteenth century to the mid-fourteenth, and it would be churlish not to admire his work here. The collection is by no means confined to Umbrian artists, but these are of course the ones to seek out. From time to time they depict the patron saint of the city, the bearded Bishop Ubaldo, about whom more later. What the Gubbians are most proud of in this art gallery are the seven celebrated Eugubian Tablets, inscribed in the seventh century BC in Etruscan and Latin with priestly rites and rules, tablets long lost and rediscovered in 1444.

The fourth side of the piazza is flanked by a massive and beautiful nineteenth-century classical building known as the Palazzo Ranghiasci-Brancaleoni, designed by Francesco Ranghiasci. Its ground floor houses shops selling the ceramics that have been created at Gubbio since the sixteenth century. They include huge plates, fired with traditional flower designs and ancient Etruscan patterns. To leave Gubbio without buying one of these superb ceramics would be a pity, though you need not necessarily buy a piece in this square, since Gubbian potters now sell their wares throughout the city.

Pottery has been created here certainly since the thirteenth century, if not before. In the sixteenth century a brilliant innovator, Maestro Giorgio Andreoli, developed techniques for producing iridescent colours, especially a flaming crimson. His skills were lost, to be rediscovered here only in 1856. The craft underwent a major revival in the 1920s, and Gubbian pottery has subsequently become world-renowned. It is undoubtedly much cheaper to buy here in the city itself than elsewhere.

Pottery is, in fact, not the only craft to have been revived in twentieth-century Gubbio. The woodworkers, whose trade dates back to a school founded by Luca Maffei at the end of the fifteenth century, now specialize in producing much sought-after stringed instruments; and today's successors of the Guild of Blacksmiths, founded in 1346, devote themselves to creating both sinuous and homely pieces of wrought-iron.

If you want to run thrice around the fountain outside the Palazzo del Bargello, descend from the piazza by the exquisite, completely medieval Via dei Consoli which runs down from the right-hand side of the Palazzo dei Consoli. The walls of Via dei Consoli contain a couple more doorways of death, and from them rise stubby old towers. Otherwise leave the piazza by the left-hand side of the Palazzo Pretorio and walk along Via XX Settembre until you reach Via Ducale, whose steps wind up to the cathedral.

Women toil to push babies in prams up the smooth centre of these steps. Cats sit on the walls and in the shade, and to the left the picturesque narrow Via Galleotti runs away back down to the city centre. Ahead the arches of the Palazzo Ducale lead into a little garden. If you turn right instead of passing through these arches, you walk up to the thirteenth-century cathedral. Its façade is not as severe as that of San Giovanni Battista, but it is severe enough, embellished only by papal insignia and by four late thirteenth-century bas-reliefs – the symbols of the evangelists, which we have come to expect, and above them Jesus as the Lamb of God.

The sheer architectural economy of the interior is breath-taking: mighty ogival arches supporting a wooden ceiling, with a later Gothic apse, frescoed in the sixteenth century to draw your eyes to the holy of holies. Of the treasures in this cathedral I especially warm to a Mary Magdalen painted by Raphael's pupil Timoteo Viti, not so much for its portrait of the reformed, sensuous saint as for the tiny orchestra of cherubs playing for her as she receives her crown of gold. One is a lutist, a second plays pipes and a third cherub scrapes a fiddle. The robust 'Deposition' by Virgilio Nucci, which we have already seen in the church of San Francesco, is matched in the cathedral by his extremely vigorous scene of the conversion of St Paul.

Opposite the west end of the cathedral is the mighty doorway of the Palazzo Ducale. This palace, on the site of a much older fortress, was begun in the 1470s by the architect Luciano Laurana (or else by Francesco Antonio Martini, for again scholars differ) on behalf of the humanist Duke Federico da Montefeltro. Federico liked people to know who was their lord, hence the numerous monograms FD (Federi-cus Dux) inscribed here and there. You can visit his palace, with its frescoed walls and magnificent fireplaces, between 09.00 and 14.00 (except on Sundays and holidays when it is either completely closed or closes at 13.00). The most ravishing part of the palace is undoubtedly the Cortile d'Onore or Courtyard of Honour, which you can always see. On three sides are cloister-like arcades, the whole finished off by a white wall surmounted by elegant brackets. These support an upper gallery, made of rose-pink bricks enlivened with Renaissance windows flanked by grey stone columns.

Walk back down the steps and turn right alongside the walls of the palazzo to follow Via della Cattedrale and reach the Palazzo del Capitano del Popolo. This rustic palace was a private house built in the thirteenth century but later bought by the city for its elected rulers. I relish the way in which it turns around a corner, its rough-hewn stones belying the delicacy of its design.

Via del Capitano del Popolo, which winds its medieval way from here as far as the Porta Castello, is narrow, shady and in my experience almost always secluded. Begonias overhang balconies, and as evening draws on lamps softly light the old street. Before you reach the Porta Castello, a street to the left takes you to two more architectural treasures of Gubbio, the church of San Domenico and the Palazzo Beni.

The church stands in the Piazza Giordana Bruno, where you can sit for a glass of wine outside an unpretentious café and imagine what the façade might have looked like had it ever been faced. If you go inside you will find a church much altered in the sixteenth and eighteenth centuries, housing a fifteenth-century terracotta *pietà* and a gorgeous Renaissance lectern made of inlaid wood. At the corner of this piazza, where it joins Via Cavour, stands the early fifteenth-century Palazzo Beni, instantly recognizable by its rusticated Renaissance doorway.

Return to Via del Capitano del Popolo and walk on to the Porta Castello, against whose ancient stones abut sweetly crumbling houses. Outside the city walls beyond the Porta Castello, Borgo Felice Damiani takes you to the fourteenth-century church of San Secondo. An earlier twelfth-century building has left us the cool and unassuming polygonal apse, which the citizens of Gubbio who live nearby use to hold up trellises entwined with vines. A brick belfry rises like a ventilator from the centre of the church. Do go inside to find the chapel of St Sebastian, which was decorated in the fifteenth century by the Gubbian painter Giacomo di Benedetto Badi, with the martyr Sebastian once more depicted in his customary role as a human pin-cushion.

If you stay outside the walls, Viale del Teatro Romano takes you as far as a little grove leading to one of the sweetest Roman theatres in Umbria, finished in the second century AD and today a children's paradise. Exquisitely excavated, the theatre is marred only slightly by the fact that when you feel like a picnic amidst its ancient stones it is usually closed to visitors. If you gain entrance, trace your fingers along the gnarled blocks of Roman stone now supported by Gubbian brick. Annually the Gubbians host ballet companies which perform here in the open air.

Continue along Viale del Teatro Romano to reach another of Gubbio's medieval gateways, the humble Porta degli Ortacci, through which you walk to find yourself once again by the church and convent of San Francesco. Walk around the west end of the church and south by the wall of the convent, cross the busy wide street and take first the Via Mazzatinti, followed by the Via Reposata, to reach the magnificent church of San Pietro.

It is not terrifically magnificent outside. As you can see from the broken-down pediments and Corinthian capitals of its façade, long ago San Pietro must have sported a marvellous Romanesque portico. On either side of the door into the church, two more porches have long since been blocked up. So has the rose window. Go inside to be bowled over by the transformation which took place in the sixteenth century. The elaborate high altar was sculpted by the brothers Antonio and Giovanni Battista Maffei. Turn round and you see rising above the west gallery the baroque organ case which they superbly sculpted and decorated at the end of the sixteenth century.

Now climb the medieval Via Vicenzo Armanni which leads from San Pietro up through an arch to the Corso Garibaldi. Here you turn right. You pass on the left the fine doorway of the fourteenth-century church of the Santissima Trinità and walk on towards the eighteenth-century statue of Bishop Ubaldo at the end of the *corso*.

Ubaldo Baldassini is the patron saint of Gubbio. A fourteenth-century house at no. 38 Via Baldassini stands on the spot where his family lived. Born into a noble Gubbian family in the mid-twelfth century, Ubaldo was orphaned at an early age and taken in by his uncle, who also happened to be bishop of this city. Ordained priest, Ubaldo was given the task of reforming the lax clerics of Gubbio cathedral and succeeded in persuading three of them to join him in the life of a monk. Together the four of them went to Ravenna to study monastic discipline, and such were Ubaldo's powers of persuasion that when he returned to Gubbio the whole cathedral chapter agreed to accept this stringent way of life.

Ubaldo longed to resign as dean of the cathedral chapter and live a completely solitary life, but his superiors insisted that here lay his true vocation. He hated the pomp of public life, however, and when the Perugians chose him as their bishop, Ubaldo hid himself from the emissaries of that city and then sped to Rome, begging Pope Honorius II to excuse him from this holy office.

The Pope granted his request, but when the see of Gubbio fell vacant two years later, Honorius himself directed the citizens to elect Ubaldo as their bishop. Ubaldo accepted the office, but no arrogance corrupted his meek self. Once some workmen intruded on his vineyards. Ubaldo mildly protested, at which the foreman threw him into a vat of mortar. Other incensed citizens took the foreman to the ecclesiastical courts, but Ubaldo himself, as the presiding judge, simply gave the miscreant the kiss of peace and set him free.

None of these virtues would have made him patron saint of Gubbio had not Frederick Barbarossa been investing Italy and had he not arrived at the city walls intent on breaching them. Bishop Ubaldo met him outside Gubbio and persuaded the emperor to desist. He last celebrated Mass on Easter Day 1160, retiring to his bed afflicted with an extremely painful illness. The citizens filed past his pallet, each taking their beloved Ubaldo by the hand. On 16 May he died. Almost immediately the sick invoked his name and were healed. Even more miraculously, Ubaldo's dead body henceforth remained incorrupt.

You can see it for yourself by driving from the Porta San Ubaldo just above the cathedral up Mount Ingino along the winding three kilometres of cypress trees which lead to his basilica. (A swifter ascent is by the *funivia* or mountain lift that sets off from close to the church of Sant'Agostino.) The medieval basilica of San Ubaldo was remodelled in 1514 at the expense of Elisabetta and Eleonora, duchesses of Rovera. Ubaldo's uncorrupt corpse was brought here in 1194 and today the saint, garbed in bishop's vesture, lies on a cata-falque, floodlit in a glass coffin.

My own guess is that Ubaldo has mouldered slightly, but not so much as to upset the faithful. In a hall nearby are kept what the Gubbians call candles, or *ceri*, huge ten-metre-long wood and canvas poles, twice swelling out like prisms in the middle and bolted to wooden stands. On 15 May, the eve of the anniversary of Ubaldo's death, they are brought down into the city. So is the corpse of the saint.

At 4.30 in the afternoon the Bishop of Gubbio and his clergy process from the Duomo with the body of St Ubaldo to bless the *ceri*. In the Piazza dei Consoli men in white trousers, red neckerchiefs and black, yellow or blue shirts bolt the *ceri* on to platforms from which protrude four handles. The statue of St Ubaldo, gleaming in his golden vestments, is set on top of one candle; a statue of St George astride his black charger and enfolded in a blue robe tops another; and a red and black coped statue of St Anthony Abbot is fixed to the top of the third. Then the yellow-shirted men hoist the candle bearing St Ubaldo on to their shoulders, the black-shirted men pick up St Anthony Abbot and the blue-shirted men do the same for St George. These mad Gubbians next race through the city at breakneck speed, bearing the huge poles and their statues, finally hurtling round the Piazza della Signoria. *En route* they rest only twice. In the Piazza della Signoria they rest a third time, before making the back-breaking ascent with the *ceri* – which are never actually lit – up to St Ubaldo's basilica on Mount Ingino.

Gubbians relish such festivities, and on Good Friday each year the laymen of the Confraternity of Santa Croce organize a solemn procession through the streets of the city, bearing a statue of the dead Jesus strewn with flowers.

From St Ubaldo's statue at the end of Corso Garibaldi a few paces up Via Dante lead you to the thirteenth-century Porta Romana. A dour tower surmounts it, its only embellishment the coat of arms of Gubbio. Through the gateway you find the twelfth-century church and former convent of Sant' Agostino, situated outside the city walls and built in the second half of the thirteenth century. Children are usually playing football outside the former cloister. Inside the church Ottaviano Nelli created a riot of fifteenth-century frescos depicting the life of St Augustine. In 1902 restorers uncovered a 'Last Judgment' painted by Nelli on the triumphal arch which precedes the apse. Whenever I visit Sant' Agostino, before I start to trace the details of these frescos I simply sit down and let their blues, pinks and reds dazzle my senses. Close to this church rises the mountain lift which takes you more easily than the road up to, and down from, the basilica of San Ubaldo. (For a trivial sum the *funivia* carries intrepid passengers from 10.00 to 13.15 and from 14.30 to 17.30.)

Return through the Porta Romana and turn right to walk up Via Nelli to the church of Santa Maria Nuova, which lies forty metres from the corner of Via Savelli della Porta and Via Dante. If you want to look inside Santa Maria Nuova, the key is kept at no. 66 Via Dante. The trouble is worth while simply for the sight of Ottaviano Nelli's masterpiece, a fresco of the Madonna del Belvedere commissioned by the Pinoli family and painted in 1413. The Virgin wears an embroidered blue robe, matched by her embroidered red dress. Her infant son is dressed in transparent lace. God the Father is about to crown her; two angels hold her train; and other angel-musicians play for her and her divine son. On either side of the fresco St Peter and St Anthony Abbot are presenting to the Madonna and child two humble members of the Pinoli family.

In the same street, closer to the centre of Gubbio, stands the seventeenth-century church of San Francesco della Pace. St Francis, with two fine churches dedicated to him in this city, is especially renowned in Gubbio because in his day an enormous wolf roamed the neighbourhood, devouring children as well as sheep. Coming across this savage animal,

Francis proved more than his match, severely admonishing the creature and then preaching to him the love of God. The weeping wolf, we are told, promised faithfully to amend his ways. Graciously Francis took the wolf's paw in his saintly hand. Since Francis had forgiven the animal its former sins, the Gubbians fed the reformed wolf for the rest of his life. Or so legend has it, and in San Francesco della Pace the beast stands on his hindlegs, slavishly attempting to curry favour with an aloof Francis who kindly offers his hand to the reformed paw.

If such a sentimental sight is not to your taste, pause for a moment before the three statues of Saints Ubaldo, George and Anthony Abbot, kept here when they are not being paraded through the streets of Gubbio during the festival of the *ceri*. Then walk speedily back to Santa Maria Nuova, turning left up Via Dante to reach the convent of San Marziale.

As its name suggests, San Marziale stands on the site of a pagan temple dedicated to the God of war. Nothing could be less war-like than this charming fourteenth-century convent and church, with a semicircular flight of steps rising up to its door and just behind the roof of the church a simple brick belfry bearing three bells to call the sisters to their offices.

San Marziale stands at the beginning of Via XX Settembre, one of the streets which runs alongside the mountain and thus does not tax one's legs. Along this street (at no. 22) is the Renaissance Palazzo Raffaelli which has been transformed into the Hotel Bosone. One of the family, Ungaro Bosone, was a friend both of Petrarch and of Dante. Among Umbria's literary 'firsts' (which, as we have seen, include the first Italian poem, St Francis's 'Canticle of the Creatures', and Jacopone da Todi's first Christmas carol), this Bosone wrote the first Italian novel, *L'avventuroso ciciliano*.

I once stayed in the Hotel Bosone and greatly enjoyed eating breakfast in a delicately decorated Renaissance salon, with *trompe-l'oeil* pilasters painted against the walls and a ceiling decorated in the eighteenth-century 'Roman' fashion. The Hotel Bosone has an excellent restaurant, but I also remember, as the rain poured down on Gubbio and swirled over the steps leading down by the hotel, the thrill of running through the drops to reach one of the trattorie in the Via Ansidei. Obviously Gubbian madness had afflicted me, as it had afflicted many others that evening, for the restaurant was full, steaming and extremely jolly. As my raincoat added to the steam, I gorged myself on *fegatelli maiale griglia*, thin slices of pigs' liver which I drenched in lemon juice.

Such rains make Umbria green. Long ago Dante himself lauded the waters of this region, the Topino, a rivulet near Assisi, and the Chiascio which flows down Mount Ingino:

> *Intra Tupino e l'acqua che discende*
> *del colle eletto del beato Ubaldo,*
> *fertile costa d'alto mondo pende,*
> *onde Perugia sente freddo e caldo*
> *da Porta Sole; e diretro le piange*
> *per grave giogo Nocera con Gualdo.*

> (Between Topino and the water that falls
> from the chosen hill of blessed Ubaldo
> hangs the fertile slope of a high mountain,
> whence heat and cold waft through Perugia's
>   eastern gate,
> while in its rear Nocera and Gualdo
> lament their heavy yoke.)

By 'heavy yoke' Dante experts surmise that the poet is referring either to the mountains near Nocera Umbra and Gualdo Tadino, or else to the exactions made of them in the Middle Ages by Perugia.

Leaving the town behind, on the way south from Gubbio to Perugia is a beautifully excavated Roman amphitheatre. Occasional flocks of sheep appear on the hilly countryside with its skyline of peaks and mountain ridges. The roadside is lined with wild roses, broom, heather and acacia trees. Poppies speckle the grassy slopes, and sometimes a farmer and his wife will be turning hay by the old-fashioned method with pitchforks. Soon the road runs along a ridge flanked by lush valleys, across which the hills rise green, with blue mountains beyond them. Half-way between the two cities is a little café rightly dubbing itself the Bar Belvedere. We begin to descend into a fertile plain and the undulating lowland just where someone has had the enterprise to build an *albergo* and restaurant.

We have, however, already seen both Perugia and Nocera Umbra, so we should rather leave Gubbio south-east by the 219 and drive for twenty-four kilometres to Gualdo Tadino, an ancient little city on the Via Flaminia. Rising on the slopes of Mount Serra Santa, Gualdo Tadino is dominated by the Rocca Flea, a fortress partly rebuilt in the thirteenth century by Frederick II and enlarged in the fourteenth and sixteenth centuries. The city's second name derives from the Roman Tadinum, and for centuries the people of Gualdo Tadino have been proud of their fine ceramics (holding a ceramics fair in July and August).

They also delight in good food, especially sausages. All Umbrians in fact relish fresh pork sausages (*salsiccie* or, as they dub the local variety at Gualdo Tadino, *soppressata*). Sometimes they make them from pigs' livers flavoured with raisins and the nuts of pine trees, and these they call *mazzafegati*.

Matteo da Gualdo, who flourished in the fifteenth century, is the town's favourite artist, and his frescos adorn the early fourteenth-century Gothic church of San Francesco which has been deconsecrated and transformed into an art gallery. I have to say that I do not hold his work equal with the splendid polyptych by Nicolò Alunno in the same church, but as if to fight back Matteo has a superb triptych, painted in 1480, in the church of Santa Maria (which adorns Piazza XX Settembre). Next to the former church of San Francesco is Gualdo Tadino's mid-thirteenth century Duomo, dedicated to St Benedict and boasting a pleasingly elaborate rose window and a well-restored late thirteenth-century high altar.

These two churches round off Piazza Martiri della Libertà, whose war memorial depicts a soldier's head nestling between a woman's ample breasts. It is hard to make out why the piazza is so haphazardly furnished with its varied establishments. Here are no fewer than three bars, naturally enough perhaps, but why two pharmacies and a barber's shop, in addition to a gunsmith whose weapons are displayed alongside the stuffed heads of a wild boar and a springbok as well as assorted innocent stuffed birds? A white clock-tower rises over the houses, topped by an octagonal brick belfry and a weather vane.

Drive north along the Flaminian Way. Sleepy Fossato di Vico is layered up the hillside, sheltering two lovely churches, San Benedetto dated 1337 and the eleventh-century San Pietro, as well as the Capella della Piaggiola which Ottaviano Nelli frescoed. Soon we reach the little town of Sigillo, whose cemetery chapel has a façade frescoed by Matteo da Gualdo and whose church of Sant'Agostino houses an 'Annunciation' painted by Ippolito Borghese in 1617. The road passes narrowly between the town hall and the church, both with belfries and bells.

Two kilometres out of Sigillo our route crosses a third-century AD Roman bridge. Matteo da Gualdo was around to paint frescos inside the next village church, Santa Maria Assunta at Scirca. Almost immediately Costacciaro crowns the next hill, still partly walled and guarded by a fragmentary Rocca. In its thirteenth-century church of San Francesco, once again Matteo da Gualdo has been at work.

We are making for Scheggia, and the route becomes even more picturesque, with green panoramas on either side, the left flank strewn with pine trees and vineyards. Scheggia was a Roman station on the Flaminian Way, yet archaeologists have dug in vain to find traces of a celebrated temple of Jove that supposedly once stood here. From Scheggia the 219 runs dizzily along a gorge and by way of the Camignano valley to bring you back to Gubbio after twelve and a half kilometres.

Pietralunga lies by a rather tortuous route twenty-three

kilometres north-west of Gubbio. Four kilometres before you reach the village you see to the left a little road leading to the eleventh-century abbey of San Benedetto Vecchio. From Pietralunga, which is still surrounded by its medieval walls, our route runs south-west to lovely rural Montone, an ancient little town set on a hill between the Rivers Carpina and Lana.

Follow Corso Garibaldi to reach Piazza Fortebbraccio and the Palazzo Communale of Montone. From here climb the steps of Via San Francesco (which offers superb views of the surrounding countryside) to reach an exceedingly fine Gothic church. San Francesco was built in the fourteenth century, and in 1514 Antonio Bencivenni made its splendid wooden doors. Of its many treasures, do not miss two late fifteenth-century frescos by Barotolomeo Carporali: St Anthony of Padua with John the Baptist and the Archangel Raphael, and a Madonna del Soccorso.

The former parish church of Montone, a Byzantine-Romanesque building of the eleventh century, boasts two more fine frescos, depicting the enthroned Madonna and the Annunciation. But none of these rival a priceless treasure (if genuine) kept in the collegiate church of Santa Maria, namely a spine from Jesus's crown of thorns, reverently displayed every Easter Sunday.

From Montone drive south to Umbértide. A fair amount of modern building has spread out from Umbértide's medieval heart, which stretches outwards from the River Tiber, but the authorities have happily kept the industrial zone far enough away not to spoil the rustic little town. Its remote origins date from a Carthaginian settlement, but Pitulum – as it was then called – was completely destroyed by the Goths. Only in 1863 did the citizens choose its present name.

A second era of regrettable military destruction occurred at the end of World War II. Today the Rocca, with its battlemented tower (built by Angelo di Cecco in 1385), and the walls which surround the domed sixteenth-century collegiate church of Santa Maria della Reggia in Piazza Mazzini, still contrast with the railway and the road which slice in two this graceful spot. Bino Sozi began building this church in the sixteenth century. Bernardino Sermigi finished its cupola in 1647. Inside, over the high altar, is a fourteenth-century fresco of the Madonna and saints.

Cross the railway and road to walk down Piazza Francesco, which seems to me less a piazza than a curving street of elegant houses with upper balconies. You reach the church of Santa Croce, next to which is the fourteenth-century church of San Francesco. Santa Croce, built in its present form in 1651, is famous for a 'Deposition' by Luca Signorelli over the elaborate baroque high altar, a painting in which the artist has exulted in brilliant swathes of red. The cloisters of the thirteenth-century San Francesco, which now house a library and cultural centre, date from the same century, stucco flaking from their brick arches where you can still see inscribed the dates when the different wings were built.

Umbértide is graced with attractively woebegone towers from which grow plants and trees. Piazza Matteotti at the other side of the railway track from Santa Croce and San Francesco is a treat, with its partly classical police station, its nineteenth-century classical post office and its medieval town hall ornamented with busts of Garibaldi and King Vittorio Emanuele II.

Noble words spoken on 6 June 1924 by Giacomo Matteotti, a socialist deputy of Parliament, are quoted on a plaque affixed to the wall of the town hall:

> *... Uccidete me ma l'idea ché è in me*
> *non la uccidere mai i.*

> (Kill me, but you can never kill
> my thoughts.)

Opposite stands another classical building with imposing round arches and pink brick forming its lower storey, the rest rising yellow and grey with an elegant balustrade. A campanile sports not just a clock but also a couple of bells and a weather vane. Brackets support the handsome lamps which softly light the square of an evening.

In hot weather I know of nothing more delightful than to sit in this piazza under an awning, or beneath one of the huge white umbrellas outside the corner bar, sipping a *caffè latte* or a *birra*, dipping into *Il Messagero*, *La Nazione* or the *Corriere dell'Umbria* bought from the newspaper kiosk opposite. The last time I was there the bar still preserved its elephant's foot toilet, a dying race in this part of Italy.

Drive north-west along the E7 from Umbértide to Città di Castello. Suddenly its thirteenth-century walls and the great defensive Porta Maggiore appear ahead. Park outside the walls and walk through the gate. The unfinished façade of the church of San Pio IX rises on your left as you take the straight and narrow Corso Vittorio Emanuele to Piazza Giacomo Matteotti, where I swear that virtually every man in Città di Castello can be found talking with his neighbour even on a Monday morning. Here is the Palazzo del Podestà, fourteenth-century in origin save for the baroque façade of 1686 which it presents to this piazza. Over to the left, beyond Piazza Matteotti, rises the cylindrical Campanile Rotondo like a thirteenth-century rolling-pin poking into the sky.

Make your way through narrow streets, criss-crossed by lanes burrowing under arches on either side, to find this cathedral and relish its coffered eighteenth-century ceiling and its pretty little organ. The dome dates from 1789, the choir from 1540. In the left transept is a famous 'Transfiguration', painted by Rosso Fiorentino.

The Duomo at Città di Castello stands on the site of a pagan temple, and its crypt – if that is the correct word – is as massive as the main church itself. Here, under a marble altar, an ancient sarcophagus houses the bones of Saints Florido and Amanzio. If you have time to visit the cathedral treasury you will discover a 'Madonna and Child', waited on by an infant St John the Baptist, painted by the master Pintoricchio.

The west door opens out on to Piazza Gabriotti, with one of

147

the exquisite gardens that are a feature of this city. Here is the Bishops' Palace, originally a twelfth-century building but today much restored. I hope that King Vittorio Emanuele III liked the moustachioed and bemedalled statue of himself (sculpted by Vincenzo Rosignoli in 1906) which adorns this square, for it seems to me unutterably pompous, and I am pleased that the letters which once announced his name have dropped out of the plinth.

Turn back in the square to admire the façade of the Duomo, the upper part medieval, the lower part sixteenth-century baroque, its swags and pilasters designed by Francesco Lazzari in 1532. Walk left into Piazza Venanzio Gabriotti (a patriot and partisan executed on 9 April 1944) to inspect its north porch and also seize on a glimpse of the sixteenth-century Palazzo Communale and the Torre Civile stubbing its finger up into the air. You can spot that Luca Signorelli in 1474 decorated it with a lovely Madonna and saints.

As the inscription on the main doorway of the Palazzo Communale states, this softly beige-coloured, rusticated building was designed in the early fourteenth century by Angelo da Orvieto and two assistants (Baldo di Marco and Bartolomeo di Gao). As he built, Angelo clearly had in mind the recently erected Palazzo Vecchio of Florence, but he also brought to this building his own special skill at exciting the onlooker by asymmetrical doors and windows. The upper part of the façade is entirely regular, but as your eye wanders down you are suddenly thrown by the way in which Angelo planned a couple of unruly doors and set them at odds, not only with each other but with the rest of the building. If you go inside you also spot a reminder of the masterly way in which Angelo deployed the staircase of the Palazzo dei Consoli at Gubbio, for here his stairway beguiles you by twisting to the right and vanishing into the upper storey of the palace.

To the right of the Torre Civile, Via dei Popolo takes you to the covered market of Città di Castello, a cornucopia of

148

cheeses, salamis, fruit, meats, vegetables, spaghetti, coffee and biscuits, which spills out into the street where stall-holders sell huge mushrooms and melons. This is the place to seek out local specialities, especially an extremely spicy *salame*, which I can tolerate only on a pizza.

If you take the tunnel opposite, which is Via delle Legue, then walk past the Campanile Rotondo and turn left down Via Luca Signorelli, you reach the early fifteenth-century church of San Domenico. On the south side is an exquisite cloister, its two-storeyed colonnades sweetly contrasting with the Gothic entrance to the refectory. The cloister is gently frescoed with scenes from the life of Beata Margherita (I wish I could discover exactly which of the many holy Margarets she is). Over the refectory door she enters paradise, hungry to partake of the heavenly banquet. In life and death she works countless wonders – the frescos depict her leaning out of heaven to help a few more souls on earth. They were painted in 1662 and restored in 1961.

Nine seats ranged around the walls allow one to rest a while in this peaceful cloister, whose well and rose garden add to the enchantment, while a brick Romanesque campanile held together by metal clamps rises above you. San Domenico itself is a typically huge Dominican church, unadorned save for more frescos and marquetry choir stalls. It takes a long time for your eyes to become accustomed to the gloom and eventually explore these gems.

Continue along Via Luca Signorelli, turn left along Corso Vittorio Emanuele and you pass the sixteenth-century Palazzo Vitelli. The legacy of the Vitelli family to this city was rich, for in the sixteenth century its members enticed here such Florentine masters as Raphael and Luca Signorelli. In the early 1520s they brought in Antonio Sangallo the Younger and the Viterban architect Pier Francesco to design their palace. Another Florentine, Giorgio Vasari, was employed to embellish the façade. Today the palace houses the municipal art gallery (open from 09.00 to 13.00 and from 15.00 to 17.30, except on holidays when it closes in the afternoon). Second only to the Umbrian National Gallery in Perugia, the Pinacoteca Communale of Città di Castello displays works by the young Raphael and by Luca Signorelli (including a fresco of St Paul, commissioned for the city tower in 1474, as well as a sensitive, slightly sexy 'Martyrdom of St Sebastian', painted over two decades later) and (in room III) a superb 'Coronation of the Virgin' by Domenico Ghirlandaio.

Piazza San Francesco opens up just beyond Palazzo Vitelli. Città di Castello's Franciscan church was built over five centuries, from the thirteenth to the eighteenth. Its early apse and doorway in no way prepare you for the splendours within. Crammed with baroque altars, with a baroque organ set behind the high altar, just as you might expect in an English Methodist chapel, the elaborately asymmetrical San Francesco scarcely exemplifies Franciscan simplicity, but it remains exhilarating all the same. The saint himself is depicted on the ceiling.

What annoys me is the way masterpieces from this church have been lifted and taken elsewhere. Over the first altar before the left transept is a reproduction of Raphael's 'Marriage of the Blessed Virgin Mary', once displayed here but now in the Pinacoteca di Brera, Milan. As if this loss were not enough, in the British National Gallery in London hangs Luca Signorelli's 'Adoration of the Shepherds', originally commissioned in 1496 for the westernmost chapel on the south side of San Francesco, Città di Castello. Happily, nobody could lift the Capella Vitelli which Vasari designed, or has taken away his 1564 altarpiece of the 'Coronation of the Virgin', and the intricate marquetry of twenty-six stalls depicting the lives of Mary and St Francis remains intact. Pietro di Ercolano made the wrought-iron grille which surrounds Vasari's chapel.

The people of Città di Castello and their guests are frequently found taking the waters at the thermal station of Terme di Fontecchio, three and a half kilometres north-east of the city. Two other excursions from Città di Castello are rewarding. One takes you along the Flaminian Way almost into Tuscany as far as San Giustino. The second takes you north-west to Citerna.

San Giustino is today a thriving industrial town which has taken care to preserve its prettiness. Castello Bufalini in Largo Pasquale is its finest monument, a castle built in 1492 and lavishly transformed by Vasari. Although the castle remains in private possession, visitors are allowed to see masterpieces by Luca Signorelli, Andrea del Sarto and Guido Reni.

San Giustino still celebrates its ancient festivals (on Corpus Christi, and on 1 June, the feast of St Giustino himself) with traditional processions and jollity. Not quite two kilometres north-east is a curiosity, the village of Cospaia which remained an independent republic from 1440 to 1826.

Citerna, again on the Tuscan border, less industrialized than San Giustino, is ancient and in Roman times was called Civitas Sobariae. The Germans savaged its Rocca in 1944, but it still towers brokenly. The fourteenth-century Palazzo Vitelli remains in excellent health. The church of San Francesco, first built in 1316, was remodelled in 1508. The style of its Renaissance interior reminds us how close we are to Tuscany, but a moving thirteenth-century crucifixion, painted on wood, tells us that we are still in Umbria. As we enter the church of San Michele Arcangelo, Florence again sheds its influence in the form of a terracotta of the Blessed Virgin Mary from the workshops of the Della Robbia family.

Drive back to Città di Castello for a meal which, if not a gastronomic treat, is certain to be an explosive experience. Visiting Città di Castello, I once stayed just outside the walls in the Hotel Europa, which has its own excellent restaurant, but one evening in the piazza housing the statue of Vittorio Emanuele III I spotted a sign announcing the Enoteca Altotiberina and promising wholesome food and local wine (*cibi e vivi locale*). So I ate there, *ai giardini pubblici*, in a cellar with shallow brick vaults and roughly plastered walls. The place was packed with parties, some tables with couples, some with just three or four friends, and with grandparents being taken out, all talking their heads off and eating at the same time.

Everything conceivably Italian seemed on offer. As an *antipasto* one could select from *prosciutto*, two kinds of salami, black bread with spicy tomato sauce and more black bread with liver pâté. For a main course some were guzzling tagliatelli and spaghetti, or pork and chips and salad. Another course with chips consisted of slices of pork, chicken, spicy sausage and another meat which I failed to identify.

Beer was available. A jug of wine, red or white, and a bottle of *acqua minerale* were plonked on the table. Eight different kinds of pizza were on offer, so I chose my favourite, *pizza capricciosa*. When it came I was puzzled as to why it contained artichoke leaves and why green olives rather than black, but I was too happy eating it to enquire, and in any case an enquiry might have seemed a criticism.

You chose the size of your pizza by specifying it in centimetres. I thought I had asked for a small one. The waiter brought me the largest I have ever eaten. I supposed it huge, until I saw the enormous platters other clients were tucking into. Finally I sliced up a jumbo piece of cheese and ate it with apples.

Before the meal ended the waiter arrived again, unasked, with a bottle of orange-brown, sweet and deadly *vin santo*, that smoky Umbrian wine made from Grechetto grapes that are said to have been hung in winter by open firesides. I paid and staggered back to the Hotel Europa, thankful that Città di Castello is not one of Umbria's hill towns.

Umbria's green and pleasant land

The mystery is that a region so tortured by strife in the past should today exude such an air of peacefulness. During the Roman empire Umbria formed the sixth region of Italy, bounded by Etruria on the west, the lands of the Sabines on the south, the Picenum to the east and on the north the Ager Gallicus. Already the region boasted great and important towns: Carsulae, Spoletium (Spoleto), Mevagna (Bevagna), Fulginium (Foligno), Nurcia (Norcia), Velsina (Orvieto), Narnia (Narni), Ameria (Amélia), Tuder (Todi), Interamna (Terni), Hispellum (Spello), Perusia (Perugia), Iguvium (Gubbio), Assisium (Assisi) and Nuceria Cammellaria (Nocera Umbra). Some of these towns, such as Gubbio, commanded important passes through the Apennines, and the Flaminian Way forged its majestic military route up through the whole region, with a spur linking it to Terni, Spoleto and Foligno.

Yet earlier the Umbrians had inhabited a much greater territory. Pliny asserted that they were the oldest of all the Italian races. In truth they probably came from prehistoric Greece. At the start of the Bronze Age this people, pouring in from the north-east, expelled from the region the Ligurians.

They found themselves up against a formidable enemy, the Etruscans, who forced many of the invaders to retreat back against the upper Apennines without, however, ever managing to force them all out of the territory. Eventually the Etuscans and Umbrians came to terms with each other, and Umbrians fought on the side of the Etruscans when they attacked Cumae in 524 BC.

Any student of this mighty, long-disappeared nation, the Etruscans, would have to visit Perugia, where the Umbrian National Archaeological Museum in Piazza Giordano Bruno takes up part of the former Dominican monastery. The Etruscan arch still stands in the city walls, and in this museum have been collected many more Etruscan remains from those same walls. Perugia has its Etruscan burial grounds, and here you can also visit the ancient tombs of the Palazzone. Even more enthralling is to leave the city by the Porta San Costanzo and take the road to Foligno to reach a superb Etruscan tomb, the Ipogeo dei Volumni, near Ponte San Giovanni. The tomb is built like a house with wings, its walls stuccoed, its ceiling coffered. It contains, however, not people but their dust, placed here in urns in the second century BC. The Ipogeo dei Volumni opens to the public each day except Mondays from 09.00 to 14.00.

Orvieto is another city rich in Etruscan remains. Stones hewed by Etruscans support the church of Sant'Andrea in the Piazza della Repubblica. Other remains include the Belvedere temple close to St Patrick's well and the Crocifissi di Tufo just outside the city. If your desire to visit thrilling Etruscan sights makes you willing to slip over the Umbrian border into Latium, leave Orvieto by the SS71 and drive towards Bolsena until you reach the ruins of Ferento, an Etruscan hill town where huge blocks of the ancient city walls survive, along with an Etruscan theatre, baths and houses. Little else remains here, for the citizens of Viterbo destroyed Ferento in 1172 for alleged heresy: the Christians there had allowed one of their artists to depict Jesus on the cross with his eyes open.

Umbrians built on the skills of this ancient, strange tribe. From the Etruscans they borrowed an alphabet of nineteen letters, like them writing from right to left. If we are to believe hostile Roman witnesses, the Umbrian people also learnt effeminacy from the same source. Yet the region's increasing prosperity was not impeded by the wars between Rome and the Etruscans. For one thing, the Romans conquered Umbria relatively speedily. Next, in spite of occasionally making alliances with the Etruscans, the Umbrians mostly preferred to side with the Romans against them, a decision that seems to have left them largely free of the savage acts of destruction of which the Romans were capable elsewhere. True, the Umbrian city of Nequinium was razed in 295 BC, but it had occupied too strategic a spot to lie dormant for long, and before the century was out rose again as the Roman city of Narnia (or Narni, to use its modern name).

When the Samnites took on Rome in 308 BC the Romans were already occupying a stronghold here. They founded another colony in 251 BC at Spoleto, and the Umbrians prudently kept out of most of the ensuing battles over the territory. Hannibal found them no help; and although for a short time they had no alternative but to make a late alliance with the enemies of Rome during the Second Punic War, the Umbrians took the earliest opportunity to make peace again. Instead of fighting Rome, they contributed soldiers to the legions, as well as two poets to Rome's pantheon: Plautus and Propertius.

The Flaminian Way helped to bring more prosperity. One of the most evocative Roman remains on the Via Flaminia is Otriculum, lying a couple of kilometres south-west of Otricoli (which itself lies sixteen kilometres south-west of Narni). Otricoli is beautiful enough, with its medieval Rocca and a church dedicated to Santa Maria which, though much remodelled, was founded in the sixth century. It houses a fifteenth-century tabernacle. Ancient Otriculum is haunted by long-dead Roman actors peopling its theatre, and by senators and their ladies taking its waters.

155

For the first time an era of stability had brought a golden glow to the land. The Umbrians traded profitably in ceramics and we even know the name of a vase-maker, M. Popillius, who set up a profitable workshop in Bevagna in the second century BC. The clays of this region, as those of Foligno and Spello, were ideal for the industry. Pliny the Elder tells us that Bevagna was walled with bricks made from clay that had been baked in the hot sun.

Veterans of Julius Caesar's legions were rewarded with plots of land in Umbria. Eventually the Romans imported a complete system of government into the region, appointing administrators to run each city. At the heart of such great cities as Assisi the central piazza still rises where once stood the Roman forum.

Under Augustus Caesar the word 'Umbria' first appeared, and the emperor here lived up to his determination to respect as far as possible the customs of the different races over which he ruled. Theatres and amphitheatres continued to be constructed. Aqueducts and baths made their appearance. Roman engineers built ponderous town walls and powerful defensive gates. At Foligno, Bevagna, Nocera Umbra and Spello, elegant Roman houses have been excavated, their mosaics now displayed for the most part in the city museums. The marble heads of Roman gods still stare blindly from the archaeological museums of Umbria, and often (as in Santa Maggiore, Spello) sepulchral pagan monuments have been given shelter in later Christian churches. The amphitheatre at Spello dates from the first century BC and three arches from the same era still support the Porta Consolare.

As the carved saints above these arches symbolize, the Romans also eventually brought Christianity, having given up making martyrs of the Christians. The bones of these martyrs, transported as precious relics up the Flaminian Way, now lie in sarcophagi in many an Umbrian church and cathedral. When the Emperor Constantine took up Christianity, Spello begged to be allowed to change its name to Flavia Constans. The emperor agreed, on condition that the people did not 'contaminate his name with deceptions or contagious superstitions'. His rescript can still be seen in the Palazzo Communale of Spello. Constantine's own devotion to the supremacy of the Christian God has been questioned, but some argue that here he was outlawing the old pagan cults of Umbria. By the fourth century over 300 communities of Christian monks, no doubt many of them tiny, were established in Umbria. Soon they were to be immeasurably enriched by the vision of St Benedict of Norcia. A century later the territory had been divided up into bishoprics and Christianity had overwhelmed the ancient faiths, a spiritual tradition renewed over half a millennium later by the devout cataclysm that was St Francis.

To me the Benedictine spirit remains its awesomely pure self not far from Umbértide on the panoramic 219 to Gubbio. After passing a couple of castles still keeping watch high in their hills, look for the signs that take you left to the Abbazia di Camporeggiano. Founded in 1060 by St Peter Damian on the site of an even older foundation, this abbey stands in as pristine condition as the day it was built. A fresco of my own patron saint, James the Great, adorns the left of the main entrance. He wears his pilgrim's hat adorned with a cockle-shell from Compostela, and carries his pilgrim's staff and purse as well as a rosary. Sporting a red beard, he looks extremely handsome. The shallow apse is cool and yet some-how stamped with a high aura of Christian culture. Perfectly proportioned arches hold up the church's one side aisle.

The unspoilt eleventh-century crypt of this abbey church once housed the corpse of St Ridolfo Gabrielli, Bishop of Gubbio, who lived higher up the hillside in Castello di Monte Cavello – today but a ruin. Even the piscina of this crypt is in immaculate condition. And the holy house is still in use as a church. Climb the steps of the main church, which is dedicated to St Bartholomew and was restored in 1971, up to its simple altar. On the days when they abjured meat, monks lived off fish, and you can still buy juicy fish nearby, caught in the tributary of the River Tiber beside which the abbey was built.

Small wonder that Benedictine spirituality could calm even the wild Lombards. In 749 one of their kings, Ratchis, went so far as to abdicate so that he might end his days at Montecassino.

The achievement of Rome had thus not been lost in Umbria, but its cultural life – save for the Christian faith – was virtually wiped out, first by the Goths and then by the Lombards. In 535 the Eastern emperor Justinian decided to fight back and his general, Belisarius, began a gradual reconquest of Italy. In 553 Belisarius's successor Narses finally drove the Goths across the Alps.

The sway of Byzantium thenceforth lasted barely twenty years, broken by the Lombards who dominated Umbria from the sixth century AD for the next four centuries. Most of Umbria was incorporated into the Duchy of Spoleto, and yet that mysteriously serene Byzantine element in Umbrian art and architecture kept its toehold, indestructible even by the Goths.

Pipin the Short and Charlemagne offered the duchy of Spoleto and its Umbrian subjects to the revived papacy. Slowly, under powerful lords, city states gained some independence, only to face another threat in the twelfth century from the attempt of Frederick Barbarossa to assert his imperial rights throughout Italy. His own officials, he planned, would control the independent, formerly Lombard cities. Both the papacy and the cities of Umbria were a match for him.

Though Barbarossa savaged Spoleto (and in reparation gave the city the icons which you can still see in its cathedral), for the most part the emperors were not despoilers of the Church or of Umbria. At Foligno Frederick II is honoured with a vigorously carved portrait of himself on the cathedral façade facing Piazza della Repubblica. Yet the feud between Guelph and Ghibbeline, emperor and Pope, split many an Umbrian city and made them continually squabble and fight among each other. At the same time divided masters allowed city communes to emerge, with Perugia dominant among them. New families struggled to positions of power and then made themselves rich.

The ascendancy of the Mondaldeschi family around Orvieto is matched by that of the Gabrielli family of Gubbio and the Trinci of Foligno. The great cities did not give way easily to these upstarts, and in the late fourteenth century the rich city of Gubbio several times rebelled and threw out its would-be seigneur Gabriele Gabrielli.

The medieval Umbrian peasant and lease-holder must often have been bewildered at the allegiances of his masters. From time to time, for instance, he was lorded over by representatives both of the Pope and the French, especially if he lived near the border with Tuscany. Monte Santa Maria Tiberina, for instance, lies eleven kilometres from the Tuscan border on the route to Umbria from Arezzo. A pre-Romanesque altar frontal in the parish church of Santa Maria bespeaks the antiquity of this panoramic spot. The remains of its castello derive from the sixteenth century. But soon it was in the gift of the Bourbons.

Beautiful Castel Viscardo supplies another example. Twelve and a half kilometres north-west of Orvieto, this village of farmers is quintessentially Umbrian, but if you look inside its parish church you will find on the high altar a silver crucifix given by *le roi soleil*, Louis XIV (not to speak of a standard captured from the Turkish fleet by the Venetians).

Castel Viscardo was a fief of the Mondaldeschi family. The same family also claimed sovereignty over the little towns between Orvieto and Arezzo, such as Ficulle on its hillock – walled during the Middle Ages, its souls cared for since the twelfth century by the parish priests of Santa Maria Vecchia, its architecture enriched in the sixteenth century by the church of Santa Vittoria, which was designed by the swaggeringly brilliant Ippolito Scalza. Without the Mondaldeschi such commissions would scarcely have been within the means of the poor peasants of Ficulle; and no doubt these little towns and villages were sometimes defended by the noble families who rack-rented their underlings. Yet to the south of Ficulle, at nearby Castello della Sala, rises a cylindrical fourteenth-century refuge tower which would have protected a Mondaldeschi in time of attack but would certainly have excluded his miserable feudal peasants. Even so, the visitor today can forget the selfish cruelties of the past and simply exult that here, and further north at Montegabbione and Piegaro, the romantic medieval castles and churches of these lords still stand.

The return of the papacy from exile in France brought changes in the architecture of Umbria (whose effect we have already discerned in earlier chapters), for in 1353 Cardinal Albornoz arrived to set about consolidating papal power. His task involved building powerful castles. As the Rocca at Spoleto testifies, brilliant architects such as Matteo Gattapone were on hand to design them. Albornoz and his papal masters also brought a new spurt of cultured life to Umbria. In Foligno, for instance, his political supporters, the Trinci family, now dominated the city for two centuries. They supported humanists such as Francesco Frezzi, a writer whose *Il Quadriregio* reveals his great admiration for Dante. In 1472 Foligno presided over a milestone in Dante's own literary history when one of its printers produced the first printed edition of his *Divine Comedy*.

Ugolino Trinci was the greatest patron of the arts in this cultivated family. Among the scholars gathered around him was the humanist Francesco da Fiano, who spent his time collecting the archaeological remains of classical Rome. Contemporary Rome surfaced here in the busts by Bernini, which the Trinci commissioned for the cathedral. Its shimmering high altar, a copy of Bernini's in St Peter's, Rome, is a noble compliment from Foligno to the papacy itself.

Between 1389 and 1407 Ugolino Trinci was deploying part of his family fortune in buying up medieval buildings in Foligno and restoring them. Eighteen years were needed to restore the family seat, still known today as the Palazzo

Trinci. The family hired the Gubbian master Ottaviano Nelli to fresco the entire chapel.

Now the artists patronized by the Trinci came into their own, men such as Giovanni di Corraduccio, Bartolomeo di Tommaso, Pierantonio Mesastris Tommaso and Pietro di Giovanni Mazzaforte. The last was the father-in-law of Nicolò di Liberatore, known oddly as 'l'Alunno' (which means 'pupil'), for he was greater than all the rest. The works of these masters hang in the Palazzo Trinci (which opens in summer from 09.00 to 12.00 and from 16.00 to 18.30, opening and closing two hours earlier on winter afternoons and not opening at all on the afternoons of Sundays and festivals). Do not miss here Alunno's arresting depiction of St Francis receiving the stigmata.

In the fifteenth and early sixteenth centuries Cesare Borgia and Pope Julius II strove to increase the sway of the Church over Umbria. In 1540 Perugia finally submitted to Pope Paul III, whose standard-bearer, Pier Luigi Farnese, brought an end to its valiant attempt to survive as an independent city state. Almost all Umbria returned contentedly to the fold of the papal states until 1798, when for two short years she became part of the Roman Republic. Napoleon took her from the papacy in 1808. But Bonaparte's harsh treatment of Pope Pius VII deeply incensed the Catholic peasants of Umbria, and they joyfully welcomed the restoration of papal rule in 1814.

I love reading the generous attempt of that staunch English Protestant historian George Macaulay Trevelyan, writing in the early years of this century, to explain what he dubbed the 'strange beauty and pathos' of this loyalty to Rome:

The men and women of the Umbrian Apennines who, bent with toil and withered by starvation and poverty, tilled the hills of olive and the valleys thinly clad with vines, or staggered down under burdens of brushwood from the grey mountains above ... what did they know of liberty, or what was it to them if Italy bled? They did not suffer from spies, for they had no politics. The censorship was no grievance to them, for they could not read. The priest was lord of their lives, but he was their only visible friend.

Trevelyan held the somewhat prejudiced opinion that 'the Catholic Church tends by its general influence to keep people poor and ignorant', but he conceded that it also 'knows how to sweeten ignorance and poverty'. As he put it, in the midst of these Umbrian peasants 'one poor priest and one poor church remain[ed] as their only help, the only symbol of the larger world outside, and of ages not absolutely prehistoric'.

Trevelyan was right. The humblest Umbrian must have insensibly imbibed a feeling for great art as he assembled in the exquisite churches of the region. No doubt he was never allowed to enter, say, the Baglioni chapel in Spello, but he could marvel at the extraordinary nimbus of divine mystery which Pintoricchio managed to impart to the decorations commissioned by the powerful Baglioni family in 1501.

The legends of saints from the misty past, the lineaments of unseen heavenly protectors, even the very face of the Mother of God herself were gloriously splashed across acres of church walls. In tiny villages such art could, and still can be, found not in one church but in two or even more. As we have seen, to mention only one example, Calvi dell'Umbria, which dominates the Tiber valley thirteen kilometres south of Narni, vaunts no fewer than three precious churches as well as a Franciscan convent, yet even today fewer than 2,500 people live here.

Even so, in spite of the influence of the Church, Perugia rose against the papacy in the heady days of the Risorgimento. The revolt was bloodily put down by the Pope's foreign mercenaries. The Italian patriots avenged this massacre the following year, and the city was relieved. From here a detachment set out to take the garrison of Spoleto. One of the bizarre consequences of this war of liberation was that Irish and Franco-Belgian soldiers were defending the Rocca there on behalf of the papacy. They fought sacrificially and vainly against the troops of Vittorio Emanuele III.

Let me quote G.M. Trevelyan again.

There is all history's profoundest irony and pathos in this tussle for an old fort 'in a gash of wind-grieved Appennine'. What quarrel lay between the Piedmontese and the men of Munster that they should have come together in this place of all others to carve each other to mutton? Or what did it profit the peasant of Connaught as he dug his potatoes and paid his rack-rent, that the vine-dressers of Umbria should remain enslaved and without fatherland? It is a strange thing, this crossing of sea and land by these Irish, to die for a Monsignor-Governor of Spoleto, bayed in the last lair of his tyranny.

So in 1860 Umbria was taken over by Sardinia-Piedmont, to be incorporated into the Kingdom of Italy the following year. In spite of an attempt to industrialize the region (notably by the founding of an arms factory and then a steel works at Terni), little changed in the harsh lives of the Umbrian peasant farmer and his family. By the end of the century over half of the people of Umbria could still neither read nor write.

For centuries the lives of most of them had been bleak. Share-croppers, some of whose dovecots and isolated homes can still be seen in Umbria, eked out a miserable living. In country villages lived the farm labourers and a few lease-holders. The ruling classes appropriated to themselves vast estates, leaving the poor to subsist on cereals or hemp, with olives bringing a little more sustenance on the mountain slopes and hills. The climate in the seventeenth century proved particularly vicious, with droughts devastating livestock and withering crops in 1614, 1645, 1655 and 1658, followed in the late 1660s and early 1670s by a series of disastrous winter frosts and atrocious spring weather.

Yet the great landowners continue to tax the poor, building themselves superb palazzi. Sixteen kilometres south-west of Perugia, for instance, at the village of Castel del Piano an avenue of trees leads to the sumptuous Villa Aureli, which was inherited by the Aureli family in the early seventeenth

163

century. While peasants starved throughout that disastrous century, the family was busy enlarging its property here and creating a terraced garden. From the mid-eighteenth century Sperello Aureli brought from the cathedral of Perugia a priest-architect named Costanzo Batta and employed him to re-model the interior of his home. Batta transformed it into a rococo palace. Today you can visit the palatial terraced gardens on Monday, Wednesday and Friday mornings.

This pattern of domination is well displayed at Gualdo Cattaneo, a hill village reached by a winding, olive-clad route that runs south-west of Bevagna for seven kilometres. The medieval walls remain, studded by towers. The church, though rebuilt in 1804, has blessed the villagers for six centuries. Its crypt dates from the thirteenth, and a beautiful fourteenth-century tabernacle is still intact in the main church. In Piazza Umberto I rises a huge cylindrical tower. It was erected in 1494 to assert the authority of Pope Alexander VI. And over the whole village lords the baronial palace, abrasive save for its graceful flight of steps and fountain.

For most Umbrians farming continued to be a hazardous occupation throughout the nineteenth century, while the fortunes of small craftsmen, tanners and the millers of oil and flour ebbed and flowed. This is the reason, I think, why we have in this book so frequently seen a revival of traditional handicrafts in recent times. Earlier traditions had died out simply because the profits from these crafts could not feed the families of the men and women who followed these trades. That they flourish today is a symbol of Umbria's present happy fortune. As you can see simply by visiting the Pinacoteca at Deruta or, better still, the church of the Madonna di Bagno at nearby Casalina, which houses 605 majolica votive tiles, exquisite majolica has been created at Deruta since the early sixteenth century. Today its factories employ ceramists from all over Italy to produce new designs alongside their ancient turquoise, yellow and green patterns. In Orvieto – where ceramics have also been made since the sixteenth century – the mouths of tourists water over the animals and leaves and pine-cone patterns on the ivory surfaces of jugs and platters. Gualdo Tadino, Gubbio and Città di Castello vie in excellence with these centres.

Woodworking always had patrons in churchmen and nobles. Today the art flourishes with new vitality. Skilled weaving is another craft that was virtually dead, to be born again at Perugia, Assisi and Montefalco, while lace-making once more thrives in Orvieto and Norcia. Around Lake Trasimeno, where woodworkers have always had to construct flat-bottomed boats, a new industry has grown up from weaving the rushes and reeds into wickerwork and chairs.

In the nineteenth century Mazzini and his republican followers declared themselves appalled at the evil diet of the poor and their susceptibility to tuberculosis and rickets. As the twentieth century began, growing social tensions emerged in the larger towns and cities.

A number of Umbrians now began to organize themselves into trade unions, and Socialists began to score in elections. In the 1920s Fascism appealed to others. But neither group could cope satisfactorily with the economic crises that sorely affected Umbria from 1929 onwards. Umbria remained a poor land until World War II, although the peasants were at least now eating good breakfasts of dried beans. Beef or meat appeared on the tables of the better-off perhaps once a week, chicken no more than five or six times a year. The tradition was to eat as much as possible, whenever possible.

Parts of Umbria, especially around Terni and Foligno, suffered hideously from bombardment during World War II. Then the post-war years saw a slow climb to prosperity. Today over 40 per cent of Umbria's working population earns a living from industry. Umbria began to exploit her rivers to provide energy and was delighted to find herself exporting it even to Rome. The textile industry revived. New roads and railway lines were built. Businessmen and tourists found themselves able to fly by jet to Milan from San Egidio airport, Perugia, in an hour. The new roads enabled more tourists and businessmen to drive to Rome and its airports within a couple of hours.

Two examples taken at random will suffice to show how cunningly the Umbrians have hidden their new industries between the interstices of their medieval villages. Sellano, on the 319 north of Borgo Cerreto, is now noted not just for its agriculture but also for its metalwork, nails, files and such-like. But all you notice is the heavenly church of the Madonna della Croce just outside the town, built in 1538. Stroncone, nine kilometres south of Terni, offers the same relaxing phenomenon: an agricultural-industrial village, specializing in mechanical engineering and plastic, but presenting to the visitor smiling olive groves, medieval walls and towered houses. Stroncone's peaceful aspect belies its history. In the Middle Ages its citizens battled with the forces of Narni, who destroyed the parish church. (It was rebuilt in 1215 at the express command of Pope Innocent III.) And in 1799 the French had to besiege this minuscule spot for sixteen days before the villagers capitulated.

Late twentieth-century Umbrians, realizing the enormous potential of tourism, have managed to infiltrate their industries into the region like invisible ghosts, so that with singularly few exceptions both the countryside and the great cities remain utterly unspoilt. Umbria is today like a jewel in the navel of Italy, its colour emerald green.

Almost the whole of its long history I find ravishingly encapsulated by driving north from Spoleto along the Flaminian Way to the temple of Clitunno. Look out for Campello Alto on your right, rising like a cream cake on its hill. Little houses rest against its buttressed walls. Barnabite monks once inhabited a convent here, and their tiny church possesses a totally unexpected baroque altar and tabernacle. Nearby rises the Castello di Lenano.

Every vista is one of terraced olive groves climbing to the mountains. Though you would scarcely guess it, here too – as well as tobacco plantations – are to be found some of Umbria's modern industries, metalwork and plastics, cleverly concealed in the landscape. As you approach Clitunno the medieval ruins of Pissignano tumble down the hillside. The derivation of its name bespeaks its antiquity – 'piscina Janis', a holy spring dedicated to the two-faced Roman god Janus.

Virgil and Pliny the Younger both praised the beauties of Clitunno and its river. Clitumnus, after whom the river is named, was also a god, consulted here by no less a personage than the Emperor Caligula. Here stands, however, not a pagan temple – though it looks like one – but one of the earliest Christian shrines, the Tempietto di Clitunno, dating back as far as the fourth century. What is more, the Christians who colonized the pagan shrine had not the slightest compunction at incorporating in their church its pagan stones.

To visit the Tempietto, look for the signs taking you to a little gate, where, if you arrive between 09.00 and 12.00 or 16.00 and 19.00 (18.00 in winter), the custodian will let you in. The Tempietto is closed on Mondays and in the afternoon on Sundays and festivals. Today the Tempietto is dedicated not to the river god but to the one who displaced him, San Salvatore, and inside you can just make out two remarkable eighth-century frescos depicting Jesus the Saviour and Saints Peter and Paul.

Just as the Umbrians still use the pagan name for the Tempietto di Clitunno, so they still laud the magical virtues of the Clitunno spring, which rises close by amidst weeping willows and poplars, and swells into a swan-decked lake. In the nineteenth century the great poet Giosuè Carducci composed an ode in its honour. Drinking its water, Umbrians still insist, renews one's youth.

What strikes me here as a sign of Umbria's brilliance in welcoming the age of the intelligent tourist is the way that a fifteenth-century mill, the Vecchio Molino, standing virtually opposite the Tempietto, its ancient stones once driven by the Clitunno waters, has been sensitively transformed into a superb hotel.

First-class hotels and humble restaurants throughout the region have profited from the lush development of Umbrian farming. If you eat out in Umbria of an evening, take care to arrive around eight o'clock or, if the summer is hot, perhaps at nine. The kitchen will almost certainly close an hour later. The food will vary region by region. Even simple *minestrone alla contadini* will depend on the local vegetables for its special kick. Ribbons of pasta (*fettucini*) will be served in one place with truffles, in other places with giant, succulent mushrooms. The meat and powerful gravy of a wild boar in season will be soaked up with noodles (*pappardelle*) in one restaurant, while elsewhere in the region the chef will be offering *pappardelle alla lepre*, that is, with a hare sauce.

Wherever you eat, the meal will be served with charm, the kind of charm that was shown to me by the family of Mario Bocciani on their farm outside Assisi. Sometimes my Italian goes awry, as once it did under the influence of that wine known as 'Sagrantino di Montefalco', which can match and even better the taste of a wild boar, let alone my brains. On that occasion I must have misunderstood the word for truffle, for without a word the waiter smilingly sped to my table with one of those sensitive, subtle funghi between his fingers, to show what he was offering with the meal.

That was courteous enough, but I can cap the story. My wife and I once sat dining in an Orvietan restaurant outside the main tourist season. Only four American visitors, all of them women, were eating there besides us. They were not only richly savouring their meal but also giggling with pleasure at the attentions of the waiter, who nevertheless in no way neglected us at our corner table. On every table was a vase of roses. As the women left, one bent down to sniff a rose. Elegantly the waiter, who was holding open the door for her, plucked the rose from its vase and handed it to her. In a trice, before the other three Americans had managed to cross the threshold, the head waiter flew across the room to present each of them with another rose. They left entranced, and I marvelled at Umbrian charm.

Practical information

The Magic of Italy is based in Britain at 47 Shepherd's Bush Green, London W12 8PS (reservations tel. 01-743 9555; brochures tel. 01-749 7449), and in Umbria at Promotour, Via Pievaiola 11, Perugia (tel. 075 756845).

The Italian National Tourist Board in London is at 1 Princes Street, London W1R 8AY (tel. 01-408 1254).

The Azienda di Promozione Turistica, Perugia is at Via Mazzini 21 (tel. 075 25341), and the tourist office is at Corso Vannucci 4a (tel. 075 23327).

The Azienda Autonoma di Soggiorno e Turismo at Gubbio is at Piazza Oderisi 6 (tel. 075 9273693), as is the tourist office.

The Azienda di Promozione Turistica of Assisi is in the Palazzo del Capitano del Popolo in the Piazza del Commune (tel. 075 812450), and the tourist office is at Piazza del Commune 12 (tel. 075 812534).

The Azienda Autonoma di Soggiorno e Turismo at Spoleto is at Piazza della Libertà 7 (tel. 0743 49890).

The Azienda Autonoma di Soggiorno e Turismo of Orvieto is at Piazza del Duomo 24 (tel. 0763 35562) and the tourist office is at the same place (tel. 0763 35172).

The telephone number for information and bookings at San Egidio airport, Perugia is 075 698447.

Travel agencies in Umbria

ASSISI

Cosmoviaggi
Via Ancajani, 06081 Assisi
Tel. 075 812234

Franciscus
Via Piaggia S. Pietro 9,
06081 Assisi
Tel. 075 8133006

Mavitur
Via Frate Elia I/B,
06081 Assisi
Tel. 075 813083
Telex: 661090 MAVI I

Stoppini
Piazza Santa Chiara 4,
06081 Assisi
Tel. 075 812597
Telex: 660115

Pellegrinaggi Porziuncola (B)
Via G. Becchetti 5/A, 06088
Santa Maria degli Angeli
(Assisi)
Tel. 075 819523

BASTIA UMBRA

Europasette Viaggi e Turismo
Via S. Angelo 14,
06083 Bastia Umbra
Tel. 075 8003366

CASCIA

Casciana (B)
Via Roma n. 4, 06043 Cascia
Tel. 0743 71147

CITTÀ DI CASTELLO

Gestioni Turistiche S.p.A.
Via C. Liviero n. 2/H,
06012 Città di Castello
Tel. 075 854333

Agevico (B)
Piazza Garibaldi 6,
06012 Città di Castello
Tel. 075 852384

FOLIGNO

**Fabrizio Mariani Viaggi e
Turismo**
Corso Cavour 135,
06034 Foligno

Tel. 0742 53830–54589
Telex: 661012 MARNEG 1

Vic Travel
Via C. Battisti, 06034 Foligno
Tel. 0742 60613

Visetur (Filiale)
Via Chiavellati 10/A,
06034 Foligno
Tel. 0742 50362

GUALDO TADINO
Tadino Tourist Travel
Piazza Garibaldi 15,
06023 Gualdo Tadino
Tel. 075 913912

GUBBIO
Mondial Clipper
Piazza S. Giovanni 15,
06024 Gubbio
Tel. 075 9271748

Il Bucchero (B)
Via Ubaldini 22, 06024 Gubbio

NARNI
In viaggio
Piazza Cavour 7, 05035 Narni
Tel. 0744 726143

ORVIETO
Fabbri Viaggi
Via Del Duomo 58,
05018 Orvieto
Tel. 0763 33448

Pinpoint Travel Agency
Via L. Signorelli 2,
05018 Orvieto
Tel. 0763 32555
Telex: 222385 COOT 1

PERUGIA
Acitur Umbria
Via M. Angeloni 1,
06100 Perugia
Tel. 075 754748
Telex: 661121 ACITUM 1

Aia Tour
Via XX Settembre 51,
06100 Perugia
Tel. 075 22929
Telex: 66177 SEGAIA 1

Compagnia Italiana Turismo (CIT)
Corso Vannucci 2,
06100 Perugia
Tel. 075 26061

Consul Travel
Via Sicilia 11, 06100 Perugia
Tel. 075 75144–72841
Telex: 600308 CONSUL

Gestioni Turistiche S.p.A. (Filiale)
Via Mazzini 16, 06100 Perugia
Tel. 075 24849

Grifoviaggi
Via Bonazzi 33, 06100 Perugia
Tel. 075 24481

Heart Green Viaggi e Turismo
Corso Cavour 115,
06100 Perugia
Tel. 075 62234

Italspring
Via U. Rocchi 4,
06100 Perugia
Tel. 075 62000
Telex: 661159

Perusia Viaggi
Via F. di Lorenzo 10,
06100 Perugia
Tel. 075 66146
Telex: 661152 VILMN-1

Tuttoturismo
Viale Indipendenza 3,
06100 Perugia
Tel. 075 61841
Telex: 600320 TOTUR 1

Tuttoturismo (Filiale)
Via Pievaiola 13,
06100 Perugia
Tel. 075 61841
Telex: 600320 TOTUR 1

Visetur
Piazza Italia 12, 06100 Perugia
Tel. 075 20249
Telex: 660064

SPELLO
Ispellumtour
Piazza Matteotti 3,
06038 Spello

SPOLETO
Deux mondes Viaggi
Via Fornari 2, 06049 Spoleto
Tel. 0743 40638

Umbria Viaggi
C.so Mazzini 19, 06049 Spoleto
Tel. 0743 46642

TERNI
Apatan
Via Pacinotti 19, 05100 Terni
Tel. 0744 49225

Interamna Tours
Via Mazzini 21, 05100 Terni
Tel. 0744 57057

I Viaggi del Drago
Via Lungonera Germinal,
Cimarelli 2 A, 05100 Terni
Tel. 0744 52518

I Viavai di Vevi
Via A. Volta 8, 05100 Terni
Tel. 0744 46949–46940
Telex: 661054 VIAVA 1

Rovide
Corso Tacito 12, 05100 Terni
Tel. 0744 54528

Spazio e Tempo Libero Viaggi
Via I Maggio 13, 05100 Terni
Tel. 0744 59679

Tiva
Via Becaria 9, 05100 Terni
Tel. 0744 59146

TODI
Tiva
Piazza del Popolo 14p,
05100 Todi
Tel. 075 882161

(The telephone numbers given above are those used when calling within Italy. For calls from the UK replace the initial zero by 010 39.)

Bibliography

James Bentley, *A Calendar of Saints*, Orbis Books, London, 1986.

Bernard Berenson, *Italian Painters of the Renaissance*, Oxford University Press, Oxford, 1932.

Marcus Binney, 'Villa Aureli, Umbria, the home of Count Leonardo di Serego Alighieri', *Country Life*, vol. CLXXIX, no. 4619, London, 27 February 1986, pp. 496–501.

Cesare Brandi and Folco Quilici, *Umbria*, Silvane Editoriale d'Arte, Milan, 1976.

E. Bucciotti, *Visioni di Perugia*, De Agostini Editori, Novara, 1980.

E. Camesasca, *Tutto la Pittura di Perugino*, Rizzoli, Milan, 1959.

E. Carli, *Il Pintoricchio*, Electa, Milan, 1960.

Romeo Cianchetta, *Assisi*, Plurigraf, Narni-Terni, 1986.

Dario Giorgetti, *Umbria: itinerari archeologici*, Newton Compton Editori, Rome, 1984.

Ottorino Gurrieri, *Perugia*, Plurigraf, Narni-Terni, 1985.

Mary A. Johnstone, *Perugia and Her People*, Grafica Editori, Perugia, n.d.

David Knowles, *Saints and Scholars. Twenty-Five Medieval Portraits*, Cambridge University Press, Cambridge, 1962.

C.H. Lawrence, *Medieval Monasticism: Forms of the religious life in Western Europe in the Middle Ages*, Longman, London, 1984.

Francesco Federico Mancini and Giovanna Casagrande, *Perugia*, Fotometalgrafica Emiliana, Bologna, 1985.

Bibliography

A. Martindale, 'Luca Signorelli and the Drawings connected with the Orvieto Frescoes', *Burlington Magazine*, vol. CIII, London, 1961, pp. 216–20.

F.J. Mather, 'Giotto's St Francis series at Assisi Historically Considered', *Art Bulletin*, no. XXV, New York, 1943, pp. 97–111 and 368–70.

Millard Meiss, *Giotto and Assisi*, University of New York Press, New York, 1960.

Alberto Melelli, 'L'altopiano de Castelluccio', *Attreverso l'Italia: Umbria*, Touring Club Italiano, Milan, 1984, pp. 263–9.

J.R.H. Moorman, *The History of the Franciscan Order from its origins to the year 1517*, Oxford University Press, Oxford, 1968.

J.R.H. Moorman, *St Francis of Assisi*, SCM Press, London, 1950.

Giusta Nicco Fasola, *La fontana di Perugia*, Rome, 1951.

B. Nicholson, 'Again the St Francis Series', *Art Bulletin*, no. XXVI, New York, 1944, pp. 193–5.

John Pope-Henessy, *Italian Gothic Sculpture*, Phaidon, Oxford, 1986.

C.J. Roettger, *Saint Benedict and His Times*, St Louis, 1951.

Pierluigi Ronchetti *et al.*, *Umbria*, Fratelli Fabbri Editori, Milan, 1974.

L. Shirley-Price, tr., *The Little Flowers of St Francis*, Penguin Books, Harmondsworth, 1959.

Alberto Sorbino, 'Gli ex-voto della Madonna dei Bagni el la ceramica di Deruta', *Attreverso l'Italia: Umbria*, Touring Club Italiano, Milan, 1984, pp. 98f.

Mary G. Steegman, tr., *The Book of Divine Consolation of the Blessed Angela of Foligno*, Chatto & Windus, New York, 1909.

M. Sticco, 'Jacopone da Todi', *Letteratura italiana*, vol. 4v, Milan, 1961–2, 1: pp. 129–57.

Leonetto Tintori and Millard Meiss, *The Paintings of the Life of St Francis in Assisi*, New York University Press, New York, 1962.

Bruno Toscano, Luciano Giacche, Lamberto Gentili, Bernardino Ragni, *Itinerari Per l'Umbria*, Editoriale l'Espresso, Rome, 1983.

Touring Club Italiano, *Guida d'Italia: Umbria*, 5th edition, Milan, 1978.

G.M. Trevelyan, *Garibaldi and the Making of Italy*, Longmans, Green and Co., London, 1911.

Bibliography

G.M. Trevelyan, *Garibaldi's Defence of the Roman Republic*,
Longmans, Green and Co., London, 1907.

Evelyn Underhill, *Jacopone da Todi, Poet and Mystic*, J.M. Dent
& Sons, London, 1919.

Ada Urbani, *Profumo di Tartufo*, Forte Editori, Florence, 1983.

John White, *Art and Architecture in Italy 1250–1400*, Penguin
Books, Harmondsworth, 1987.

John White, 'The Reliefs on the Façade of the Duomo at
Orvieto', *Journal of the Warburg and Courtauld Institutes*, vol.
XXII, London, 1959, pp. 254–302.

Giuseppe Zoppis, *Gubbio. Guida Storico-Artistica-Fotografica*,
Gavirati Foto-Editore, Gubbio, 1986.

Index

Index

177

Index

Index